GARETH ARMSTRONG

Gareth has combined the roles of actor and director throughout his career. He has performed at the Royal Shakespeare Company, in the West End and at Shakespeare's Globe. As a director he founded the Made in Wales Stage Company, was Artistic Director at Cardiff's Sherman Theatre, and Artistic Associate at Salisbury Playhouse.

Following the international success of his one-man show, *Shylock*, he has specialised in solo performance and worked with writers and actors to create over a dozen new theatre pieces.

He has written and narrated radio features, spent many years in *The Archers*, and regularly records audiobooks and video games. He works with students at the Central School of Speech and Drama and as a member of the examination board of Trinity Guildhall.

He is the author of *A Case for Shylock: Around the World with Shakespeare's Jew* (Nick Hern Books), with a foreword by Judi Dench.

www.garetharmstrong.co.uk

T0386565

SO YOU WANT TO DO
A SOLO SHOW?

Gareth Armstrong

Foreword by Maureen Lipman

NICK HERN BOOKS
London
www.nickhernbooks.co.uk

A Nick Hern Book

SO YOU WANT TO DO A SOLO SHOW?
first published in Great Britain in 2011
by Nick Hern Books Limited
14 Larden Road, London W3 7ST

Reprinted in 2019

Cover designed by Peter Bennett
Author photo by Nathan Amzi

Typeset by Nick Hern Books, London
Printed and bound in Great Britain by
Mimeo Ltd, Huntingdon, Cambridgeshire PE29 6XX

A CIP catalogue record for this book
is available from the British Library

ISBN 978 1 84842 084 7

Woodland
CARBON
www.woodlandcarbon.co.uk
NICK HERN BOOKS
Printed on Carbon Captured paper

For Frank Barrie,
a gifted and generous mentor and friend

Contents

CONTENTS

Foreword

If I had read this book before embarking on either of my two one-person shows, I might now be living in Monaco, tax-free, giddy from Louis Roederer Cristal and mopping up Princess Charlene's tears before bedtime. *So You Want To Do A Solo Show?* is a thorough, meticulous, hands-on, 'how-to-do' manual, covering everything from the germination of an idea right through to the costing of the flyers. It is, I think, the most valuable read for any performer who has ever thought 'If *only* I could have some control over the way my career is going.'

Gareth Armstrong has form. He has written, directed and performed in this odd milieu, where, as Joyce Grenfell once said, 'If I put out my hand to give you something but you don't reach out to take it, the circle has not been completed.' The circle. It sounds a little *'hakuna matata'* but that's how it is with solo work, where the audience's imagination is half of the dramatis personae.

I remember being so petrified before opening in *ReJoyce*, my show about Grenfell, that no one would want to sit through two hours of Maureen Lipman *being* her, that I booked two sessions with a hypnotherapist, just to get me through opening night. She was excellent, but this book might have saved me a hundred and twenty quid.

Later, I realised that the secret of stepping into the shoes of someone who is much revered is that the audience sees you, remembers *her* and then, quite subtly, relaxes into a version of a third-person amalgam of both of you. A taxi driver dropped me outside the Duchess Theatre one night and, seeing the words 'Maureen Lipman in *ReJoyce*' on the marquee, asked, 'Who's in it wiv you then, Maureen?'

'Er… no one,' I replied lamely. 'Just me.'

''Ow long's it last then?' he persisted.

I told him it was about two and a quarter hours to which he responded:

'Gor blimey, girl – that must be bleedin' borin',' adding, for good measure, 'Don't get me wrong – I don't mean for you… I mean for the *audience!*'

Armstrong covers nerves and confidence, the strains and elation of solo work, and even gives tips on loading up and travelling after. He quantifies your costs and your supporting staff and extras, and he has input from experts in the fields of all kinds of 'small is beautiful' festivals and venues. In short, this is a valuable edition to your bookshelf – somewhere in between David Niven's *The Moon's a Balloon* and Stanislavsky – and may just inspire you to action, method and the sound of many hands clapping.

Maureen Lipman

Acknowledgements

I would like to thank the following people for making this book possible:

All the actors who allowed me to feature their shows in the case studies that appear here. They were generous with their time, honest about their experiences and infectious in their enthusiasm.

The people who for over a decade kept my solo career on the road, and thus prompted this book: Guy Masterson of Theatre Tours International, Martin Platt of UK Arts International, Richard Jordan, Emma Hands of Indigo Entertainments, and Mark Makin of makin projects, who also provided invaluable information on the logistics of setting up solo touring and its often alarming realities.

In America, Robert Friedman battled visa controls and shrinking US arts budgets to get me to the States on more than a dozen occasions, and the UK and international staff of the British Council who took on the rest of the world.

The players who are still, or soon will be touring solo shows that I have directed, and taught me so many valuable lessons: Rohan McCullough, Issy Van Randwyck, Gerard Logan, Rhodri Miles, the doyen Roger Llewellyn, and Guy Masterson who now plays Shylock in the show I wrote for myself.

The playwright Bernie Byrnes, who not only writes exemplary one-person plays but also helped me enormously with the research for the Appendices and thus made life easier for all those aspiring solo performers out there.

ACKNOWLEDGEMENTS

The Publisher and his Commissioning Editor: Nick Hern and Matt Applewhite, who encouraged the concept, identified the shortcomings, corrected the errors and still manage to stay my very good friends.

Gareth Armstrong

Introduction

'My idea of hell would be a one-woman show, I wouldn't be able to do that...'

Judi Dench (And Furthermore)

Most actors, however, at some point in their careers will think about doing a solo show. It's a very small percentage that will actually get their piece staged. A poll as to when and why actors abort their brave attempts would be very instructive. Early quitters may be put off by the responsibility, the solitary status, the sheer hard work or because an offer of more conventional work comes along. If none of these scupper your resolution, it may be money, logistics or loss of bottle. There are innumerable reasons why you'd quit, all of them justifiable, but you'd be missing a life-changing experience.

At whatever stage you are in your career, rewind to that existential moment when you decided the only life for you was on the boards. Choosing to do a solo show will remind you of the sensation of launching yourself on a thrilling adventure, it will empower you, and put you where you know you belong – centre stage. And you won't even have had to go through the agony of an audition.

One of the features that distinguishes younger actors from many of their older colleagues is an entrepreneurial spirit, born partly of the zeitgeist but also from the changes in the profession, which have diminished and curtailed the opportunities to work in live theatre. A career path for previous generations of performers was much more straightforward than it is today. After training, getting an agent, applying for Equity membership and learning how to sign–on for unemployment benefit, most young actors would have waited for the phone to ring and hoped it was an opportunity to audition for a season of work in a regional theatre. What followed was not always the effortless rise to the stardom of their dreams, and taking part-time employment in retail or an office was a frequent recourse, but the talented would generally find a network of theatres that would engage them frequently enough for them to at least identify themselves as professional actors.

Changes in theatre politics and policy have dismantled that structure and nowadays young actors realise they have to be more proactive to get work, and ruthlessly self-promoting to *keep* themselves in work. They will have developed their own websites, with links to their showreels and voice-over demos. They will collaborate with each other in forming small-scale theatre companies, take options on plays or novels to adapt into film scripts, and of course devise, commission or write solo performances.

But judging from the majority of solo shows currently on offer around the country it is apparent that most are created not by actors fresh from drama school and eager to take centre stage, but by those with a degree of experience. That experience is often a decade or more working in the profession and, as significantly, *not* working in the profession. Frustration with the trajectory of a career is one of the principal reasons for going solo. That was certainly what triggered my interest in the genre.

The actor Frank Barrie created a one-man show, *Macready*, about the great nineteenth-century actor-manager, William Macready, and toured it for twenty-five years. As well as giving him employment, it brought a degree of independence, great personal satisfaction, a clutch of awards and the opportunity to travel the world. Like many of his friends impressed by his achievement, I asked him how to go about doing something similar myself. His response, 'First find a subject you are passionate about,' is still the best piece of advice for any would-be solo performer.

Years later, whilst playing Shylock in *The Merchant of Venice*, I became obsessed with the character, and was reluctant to abandon him at the end of our short run. There was nothing as challenging on my professional horizon so I decided to devote the next year to creating a one-man show about Shakespeare's infamous Jew. I started only with the prescribed passion but I was still performing my play, *Shylock*, ten years later, and, as well as tackling another Shakespearean icon alone (Prospero in Stephen Davies's play *Dr Prospero*), I have had a hand in creating over a dozen solo plays for other performers. What I learnt from my own creative process and from nurturing others is the subject of this book. It will try and guide you through the process of conceiving, realising and presenting your solo show. It will question your motives, your commitment, your dedication and your stamina. The only element it will take for granted is your talent.

PART ONE

What's Your Motivation?

Paucity of other employment is the most likely reason that you are thinking of a one-person show, but you don't have to be desperate for work to want to launch your solo career. You may already have work that you don't find totally fulfilling. To walk the tightrope of a solo show will offer you more stimulation, an opportunity to showcase your talents and prove that you can tackle greater challenges than you are currently being offered. Fortunate enough to be under long-term contract to a major subsidised company, on a commercial tour or in a successful West End run, you may be playing small parts or understudying. It's understandable to feel yourself marginalised or unappreciated when your contribution seems a minor one, so trying out a solo piece can be good for your self esteem.

Whilst your self-advancement or self-improvement as a professional actor is probably why you are taking this route, you might have another more altruistic motive. Drawing attention to a cause, highlighting an injustice or celebrating a neglected life might be your inspiration, and your passion and commitment will be hugely to your advantage. But you have chosen to champion your cause through a piece of theatre, not a tract or a blog or a petition. Your sincerity and good intentions won't let you off the hook where a paying audience's expectations are concerned. Take a leaf from the BBC's mission statement, which is to inform, to educate – and to *entertain*.

One among many

What used to be a small trickle of solo shows from what was considered a slightly eccentric cadre of actors is now a veritable flood. Yours will have to be pretty special if it's to stay afloat. You will need to possess a degree of self-confidence somewhere beyond the courage that it takes to act at all. If going in front of an audience as a member of a cast exposes you and your talent, how much more vulnerable you are when the whole audience's attention is focused on you for the entire length of the play. Belief in yourself, and equally in your material is crucial.

Before you start the process, it's as well to confront the reality of working on stage alone. However many people are involved in getting your show on the road, it is you who will be up there speaking the first and last lines – and every line between. If something goes awry, only you can get yourself out of a tight spot. If the audience is inattentive, unappreciative, disrespectful or asleep, you have to address that situation without anyone to help you out, back you up or crack up with over a drink after the show. You are all the audience have to hold their interest, so there are no moments offstage, no gaps where you have time to refocus, recharge your batteries or even take a leak.

The relationship between the solo performer and his or her audience is unlike any other in the theatre. It is in effect a two-hander, with the audience as the other, silent player, and, whether it's love or hate at first sight, it's impossible to be indifferent to that single individual who is demanding all your attention. The number of actors who balk at the notion of performing a solo show is as nothing to the number of audience members who turn tail and run at the prospect of sitting through one. They have an aversion to the genre in the same way that some people can't stand opera or Shakespeare on stage.

If showcasing your talent in the hope of generating other work is one of your aims, the depressing fact is that casting directors are unlikely to turn up. Since going to check out actors' work is part of their brief, this reluctance may seem unreasonable, but the reality is that devoting an evening to just you will only tick one box. Going to see a full-cast show, or a student showcase, they will argue, is a much more cost-effective use of their time. Thinking of your solo show as a stepping stone to more and better work is, frankly, optimistic. It will demonstrate your resourcefulness and versatility, but these are not necessarily the qualities most employers are looking for in an actor.

You should ask yourself whether staging a show with you as the only focus of attention is a burning desire to tell a story, or an act of self-indulgence. We acknowledge that somewhere in an actor's psyche is the need to be noticed, to be appreciated, to be loved. But however deserving you are, any hint of narcissism or neediness will immediately put a barrier between you and your audience. You have to earn their attention, their appreciation and their respect. In a pecking order of importance it should be the play, the audience and, finally, you.

Rules that will apply to your performance whatever its subject matter:

- Distinguish between arrogance and total self-confidence on stage.
- Be vocally assertive without hectoring.
- Be self-deprecatory without sycophancy.
- Use open body language.
- Embrace the whole audience with your eyes.
- Make your audience laugh.
- Move your audience.
- Inform your audience.
- Surprise your audience.
- Never insult your audience's intelligence.
- Never, ever, risk boring them.

What's Your Inspiration?

Watching a fellow actor tackle a solo show may have sown the seed. You may have been inspired by the solo performances of some theatrical luminaries. Perhaps you saw Ian McKellen during the year of his life he devoted to *Performing Shakespeare*, Antony Sher in *Primo*, or Vanessa Redgrave in *The Year of Magical Thinking*. It is unlikely that any of the above did it because they needed the money (indeed, McKellen donated the proceeds from his marathon tour to AIDS charities). It's doubtful too that they did it to improve their profile or because they were short of other offers. They did it out of their passion for the work, and that showed onstage.

You may already have some idea of what story you want to tell and how you want to tell it. Your first major decision, if your play isn't already in the repertoire, will be whether to devise or write the script yourself or collaborate with a writer. If the subject matter is you, it is vital that the voice remains authentically your own. A good writer will know that instinctively. For other life stories or fictional narratives you will obviously want to work with a writer who is knowledgeable or at least engaged by the subject. And just as solo performing isn't for everyone, not all playwrights are comfortable with writing monologues.

What's Your Show?

Your show will come under one of the following ten categories:

1 A previously performed play

2 A play using your own life experiences

3 A play based on a real-life character or characters

4 A play based on a fictional life

5 A play revisiting a fictional creation

6 A play celebrating a literary life (by impersonation or in recital)

7 A play adapted from other media

8 A play for children

9 A play based on utilising a special skill

10 A play based on none of the above

1. A Previously Performed Play

This is the most straightforward choice: to reprise a performance of a play you have seen, or stage a published play that you have read. This frees you from many of the artistic dilemmas of more complex routes. If you don't already have a copy of the script you have in mind, if it is out of print or not available from a bookshop, you can try and access it via internet sites or direct from the publisher. If the script has not been published you should contact and request a copy from the playwright's agent.

If you have no definite play in mind you can search online for solo plays written by playwrights whose work you admire, the sites of play publishers or the sites of producing theatres that specialise in small-scale work or new writing. More adventurously, you could contact literary agents and investigate the availability of unpublished or even unperformed solo work. There may be a neglected gem by a writer who is as eager to be performed as you are to perform. Or a revival of a once-staged but now forgotten play could be good for you and the writer. If you are receptive to looking beyond the British repertoire then use the same resources to search out North American or Australasian plays, or European plays in translation.

An invaluable resource is the website Doollee.com which is a truly comprehensive guide to modern playwriting and English plays which have been written, adapted or translated into English since 1956. By clicking on the link to 'Characters' and specifying one male or one female actor, you will be bombarded with solo plays of every description with further links to the playwright, their known works and how to contact them.

Be sure, before you start learning the lines and rehearsing your curtain call, that the necessary rights to your chosen text are available, and that you can afford them. Another actor may have had the same idea and already taken an option on the performing rights, the playwright or his agent may not be prepared to release the rights to you, or the fees charged may be prohibitive.

Don't capitulate at the first rebuff if you get a rejection because polite and persistent approaches sometimes pay off, but ultimately be prepared to accept rejection and look for another play.

Be realistic about casting. Just because you long to play a part doesn't necessarily mean you *should* play it. Think hard about how suitable you are for the role. Canvass some opinions from friends and fellow professionals whom you trust and look out for the literal or metaphorical raised eyebrow.

CASE STUDY

Guy Masterson, *The Boy's Own Story*

Guy Masterston's name appears in this book more than once as, in one guise or another, he is responsible for more solo shows than anyone currently working in the UK.

His first foray was as an actor needing to generate his own work and searching around for a suitable scripted one-man vehicle. *The Boy's Own Story* was the first full-length play written by Peter Flannery and had premiered in Manchester. The story of a goalkeeper, bored with inactivity at a Sunday-league

---

match recounting his background, frustration and ambitions, took Guy to Edinburgh for the first of the eighteen Festivals he has attended since, and went on to tour the UK for two hundred performances. This first experience got him hooked on solo shows, and his work has subsequently grown more innovative and ambitious. Since that outing in 1991, he has performed seven, directed sixteen, and had a hand in touring over forty-four one-person shows.

His stable has been an eclectic one and has embraced virtually all the different approaches catalogued here. It's the passion and skill of the actor that he rates as pivotal but warns against the 'ego-play' as the surest way to alienate an audience. Energy, humility, sensitivity and stamina are the qualities that he rates most highly.

For his goalkeeping debut, Guy needed a large Astroturf six-yard-box goalmouth, but his most recent performances have required a single chair and imaginative but uncomplicated sound and lighting plots.

2. A Play Using Your Own Life Experiences

The actor who chooses not to work with an extant script has a different but potentially more rewarding road ahead. Telling someone else's story in the author's words is what actors do most of the time, and solo performing is a way of breaking free or at least pushing the boundaries. Your own story in your own words will be the bravest and most exposing choice of solo piece, and you will need the courage and resourcefulness of that most ubiquitous lone performer, the stand-up comedian.

Stand-ups differ from old-time comics because rather than tell a string of rehearsed jokes, they are more likely to mine their life experiences for material, and embrace a degree of spontaneity and improvisation. But if you were daring enough to contemplate that option you'd probably be reading a book called *So You Want to be a Stand-up Comedian?*... The assumption here is that your show will be prescripted, rehearsed and staged.

First impressions

Like the successful stand-up you will need to be very confident of your material, and certain that it is worth an audience's attention. But whether you tell the detailed story of your life to date, concentrate on a significant event, recall a relationship or tell a traveller's tale, no less important than your narrative is the personality you project. The audience will make up its mind within minutes about how pleased they are that they've given up an evening to hear your story.

All presentation-skills workshops begin with the alarming statistic that ninety-three per cent of how you are judged on first acquaintance is based on non-verbal information, so there's a lot riding on your entrance.

Setting the tone

Get the tone of your narrative right. Have you cast yourself as a raconteur, or is your relationship with the audience more intimate or more confessional? It will help if you *cast* your audience too. Who are they? Are they a random selection of people whom you will address as a group, or are they eavesdroppers on your internal monologue? They might represent an individual – a friend, lover, psychiatrist or arresting officer. By characterising the audience you will give yourself the familiarity of a second, albeit silent, character to engage with.

In a highly personal narrative, avoid the temptation to over-load your script with facts, figures and dates. It is not so much the 'when' and the 'where' of your life that will intrigue as your reactions to events and personalities, so edit out all but essential data. Don't feel obliged to tell your story in strict chronological order either. An audience is capable of and usually relishes the challenge of putting together a narrative jigsaw.

Past events are not necessarily best recalled using the past tense. The 'historical present tense' beloved of broadcasters ('It's 1066 and King Harold is removing an arrow from his eye…') can be much more vivid and immediate.

You will certainly need more vocal variety than you might employ in a conventional role. You know how soporific a monotonous delivery can be, so use every opportunity to change pitch and tone. Impersonating other characters within your story and giving them distinctively different voices and physical characteristics will also give you a chance to display some virtuosity.

CASE STUDY

Peter Searles, *Hey Gringo*

It was rejection that kick-started Peter Searles' solo career. When a major theatre project he was working on fell through, Peter took the £1,000 compensation payment and bought a ticket to South America to try and forget his disappointment. No stranger to vibrant experiences (he had been an oil-rigger in the North Sea before training at LAMDA), he had a wild year of adventuring before returning to life as a jobbing actor. Telling his traveller's tales to a mate in a local pub, one day the friend offered him as much Guinness as he could drink if he would retell the stories the following week to an invited audience in the bar. The anticipated fifteen minutes of local fame turned into a riotous hour and a half of unscripted anecdotes, and the same friend (actor-comedian Stephen Frost – who later directed his shows) helped get sponsorship for Peter to go to the Edinburgh Festival Fringe to capitalise on the success.

The show was a mix of storytelling, stand-up and physical theatre that got great reviews and full houses. Titled *Through Peru* it was followed a year later by *Bolivia and Beyond* and two years thereafter by *A Chile Christmas*, the last in Peter's trilogy of South American plays which are marketed under the umbrella title of *Hey Gringo*. Peter describes the shows' content as a combination of anecdote, observation and some political history, which especially in the case of *A Chile Christmas*, set in the twilight years of the Pinochet dictatorship, means that laughter is not the only reaction he aspires to achieve.

Now more formally scripted, the plays still allow for interaction with the audience and can be adapted to the size and nature of the venue. They have taken him to the Cottesloe auditorium at the National Theatre, domestic and international festivals, and even a return to their origins in the back room of a pub. After adding a fourth show, brazenly entitled *Sex with Peter Searles*, his next piece will transport the audience to India to learn of his quest for enlightenment. Relying entirely on the actor's skills, and needing no more technically than illumination and some recorded pre-show and interval music, the work represents the ultimate in self-made, totally portable theatre.

One offshoot of the success of these shows is that Peter now teaches other actors how to tell their own stories in a performance context. As well as this programme, 'The Art of Contemporary Storytelling', he has added another essential skill to pass on to actors, or indeed anyone who ever has a conversation: 'The Art of Listening'.

3. A Play Based on a Real-Life Character or Characters

While it takes chutzpah to face an audience alone, it takes even more to do so as yourself. Since hiding behind another character may be what attracted you to acting in the first place, you may be happier impersonating someone else.

Spitting image?

A close physical resemblance to a famous person, living or dead, is often the inspiration for a solo show. This lookalike factor may be the first spark, but it is not the most likely to take fire, because your one-person play has to go further than skin-deep. Walking around the National Portrait Gallery in the hope that you'll spot some likeness to a famous figure is unlikely to be sufficient impetus to create an evening of theatre.

Capitalising on your likeness to an icon will give you an initial credibility and may captivate your audience, but you will need to embody or convincingly personate some of that person's qualities to hold their attention. You might be spending a lot of time with your doppelgänger so be sure that their personality interests you more than the physical features you share.

CASE STUDY

Bob Golding, *Morecambe*

A dozen years elapsed between the initial idea and the first night of Bob Golding's show, *Morecambe*. It was his large, dark-framed glasses and more than passing resemblance to the great English comedian Eric Morecambe, together with his ability to imitate his voice that prompted the producer Guy Masterson to suggest a one-man show. A busy theatre career, backed up with lucrative voice-over work meant Bob was in no hurry to tackle the challenge, but he agreed to perform a half-hour script by his friend and fellow actor Tim Whitnall to test-run the idea in front of potential backers. Everyone invited to see the brief prototype offered to invest in the show, and the next three months were spent creating the play that conquered Edinburgh in 2009. A national tour resulted, and when the Duchess Theatre in the West End became unexpectedly available, the show played a six-week run over Christmas.

Putting a beloved national treasure on stage is a daring enterprise, and audiences are at first unsure whether they will be watching a tribute show or a play. Confusion extends to the business, too, where Bob found himself featured on the Royal Variety Performance and the show won an Olivier Award in the Entertainment category. *Morecambe* is very definitely a play, with Bob narrating the comic's life and introducing the characters who peopled it on a multipurpose set backed with the iconic red theatre tabs that featured in the TV shows. Eric without Ernie is unthinkable to fans of those record-breaking broadcasts of *The Morecambe and Wise Show* and using a ventriloquist's dummy to represent the straight man, Ernie Wise, solves the dilemma very sensitively.

Having spent three months preparing the show for no financial reward, Bob is now paid per performance, and also owns one fifth of the show in perpetuity. He plans to go on playing *Morecambe* but Bob doubts he will tackle another one-man play. Although he tours with two technicians who run the show and pack and transport the ingenious set (designed by Bob's wife Julia Bunce) in a Transit van between gigs, he misses the interaction with other performers on stage. So much so that he admits to forming attachments to his props, especially that wooden vent doll of Eric's stage partner of forty-three years. Pretending to have Ernie with him may succeed as a theatrical device but in the long term Bob would prefer a real sidekick.

Dead or alive?

An iconic living subject's life is, by definition, a work in progress, so your play will need to be nimble enough to reflect this. At the same time, you need to be aware of libelling a subject, because a litigious person could not only scupper your play but potentially also bankrupt you. Be very careful what you say, especially if you are not able to afford a lawyer to approve your script beforehand. It's not worth sacrificing whatever financial resources you have in exchange for a good laugh.

It's axiomatic that you can't libel the dead so one of them is a safer subject. Royalty, statesmen, soldiers, composers, divas, actors and even critics have all been profiled successfully. The most popular are literary lions and lionesses so they have a section to themselves later in the book.

Why a play?

With a subject in mind, ask yourself what a solo play can accomplish that a good biography or documentary cannot. A straightforward chronicle of a life might be better served in another medium, so it is your approach to that life that earns it a place on stage. You have the advantage of a beginning, middle and end to your story, but do you need to tell it in a linear way? The dates and events, the highs and the lows, are all part of the mix but in the freedom of a stage play it's possible to focus on a period, a relationship or an incident that can only in retrospect be seen to have affected your subject's life. You have the freedom not tell the whole story, but the parts of it that intrigue you and will do the same for your audience.

Get it right

Your research is all-important. Obvious sources are autobiographies, biographies, articles and the internet. With all the available information at your fingertips you can choose what to ignore, and although speculation in your script is fine if it serves the purpose of your play, factual inaccuracy is not. Get a date or name wrong and you can be sure at least one member of your audience will spot it.

More than a story

If you have chosen a well-known historical figure, hero or villain, you have the opportunity to reinforce or refute their reputation, even attempt a reassessment of that life. This approach not only increases your creative input, it also challenges your audience, makes them think, maybe provokes them. You are fulfilling the function of a good play. Coincide with a significant anniversary for your subject – then you have a useful marketing advantage too.

CASE STUDY

Rohan McCullogh, *My Darling Clemmie*

Hugh Whitemore, whose award-winning theatre plays include *Pack of Lies* and *Breaking the Code*, admits that that he finds scripting for two and more people much less problematic than for a single player. The nuances that dialogue can illuminate, the physical interaction between characters, the silences in a conversation, all add texture to a script.

I directed *My Darling Clemmie*, a play Hugh wrote for his wife, Rohan McCullough, about Winston Churchill's wife, Clementine. Hugh had done really extensive research on the Churchills and their era when writing the scripts for the Emmy award-winning films, *The Gathering Storm* and *Into the Storm*. He had been given access to previously unpublished documents, and very personal letters between Winston and Clemmie punctuate the narrative of the play, with family, domestic and financial concerns given the same prominence as great world events and judgements on the titans of the twentieth century.

It is these intimate insights that make the relationship come alive in all its complexity. Whereas history focuses on the achievements and shortcomings of Winston Churchill, the man of destiny, this play reveals him and the woman he shared his life with as imperfect parents, difficult hosts and temperamental spouses. The script and the performance illustrate Churchill's own verdict on his life: 'My most brilliant achievement was my ability to persuade my wife to marry me.'

The rehearsal process, where actress and director had unlimited access to the writer, was reassuring and challenging at the same time. It was impossible to include every element in the finished play, and as we each had differing views on which episodes were indispensable there was a degree of negotiation and occasional compromise. This stimulating creative relationship extended through the first year of the play's touring life. Minor changes to the script and the staging continued until the show played the Edinburgh Festival in 2009. Its success confounded the preconception that only the youth-oriented, the cutting-edge, the outrageous or the star-spangled succeed in that theatrical bear pit.

4. A Play Based on a Fictional Life

A monologue in character can have very modest beginnings, perhaps spawned by an anecdote of an encounter with an intriguing or eccentric personality. This can be the genesis of a whole show or, in one famous instance, a whole career. The American Ruth Draper started performing her own short monologues as a child in the drawing rooms of the wealthy New Yorkers who made up her social circle in the early twentieth century. She was styled a 'monologist', a 'recitalist' or a 'diseuse', as to call her an actress would have seemed demeaning. Five or six disparate women inhabited her shows in sketches sometimes half an hour in length and all demonstrating her perception and versatility. She went on to be a hugely successful performer for almost forty years.

She was the role model for someone still remembered and celebrated in the British theatre for her one-woman shows: her distant relative Joyce Grenfell. She too performed a series of brilliant monologues, mostly comic but some poignant, and is only disqualified from absolute solo status because she used an accompanist for the songs which interspersed her sketches. Her legacy has in turn been honoured by Maureen Lipman, who paid homage to her heroine in the show *ReJoyce*. This is much more than an impersonation of Grenfell, it is a vivid recreation of her genius through her best-loved songs, monologues and solo sketches.

The right voice and a body to match

As the character or characters who people your work are based on your own experience or imagination, you are the best qualified to find their voices. Where are they from, and what is their status? Does their voice reveal or attempt to conceal their origins? How articulate or inexpressive they are will be revealed not only in their choice of vocabulary and style of delivery, but how they interpret silence too. Their history and their attitudes will also dictate their physicality. What body language will reveal as much about them as how they speak and what they say?

Using some method

Role-playing your character, not just in the narrative context of your play, but in unrelated situations will release aspects of their personality you can feed back into your performance. Performing mundane tasks as the character will trigger a physical vocabulary too, and imagined conversations with people they might encounter on a day-to-day basis will flesh out a fully realised personality. This is not unlike a drama-school exercise when you have to stay in character for a stipulated period, but as this work is aimed at a performance outcome, you are also the chronicler, and will need to be mentally observing your actions and recording your language and conclusions in a disciplined way.

Beyond mimicry

In a sketch your voice would not need to go beyond the limitations of staying in character and telling a tale with a punchline. For a monologue – dramatic, comic or both – your script will need more texture. Beyond witnessing a convincing character study what else would an audience gain from spending time in your company? What you have to say need not be profound nor your narrative complex, but it will need some dramatic dimensions to sustain a fulfilling evening. What are the conflicts within your story? How do events change your character or characters? Part of the satisfaction an audience gets from watching a play is having to choose which version of the truth to believe, so keep them guessing as long as you can.

CASE STUDY

Alison Skilbeck, *Are There More of You?*

Alison Skilbeck, who created some of the most memorable characters in Alan Ayckbourn's plays at Scarborough, now tours a show, written by herself, that owes much to Ruth Draper's tradition as well as her playwright mentor. Called *Are There More of You?*, it portrays, in four monologues, the lives of very different women across the spectrum of age, class and nationality. Like Ayckbourn, Alison explores their characters and painful dilemmas through humour, and although the only thing they appear to have in common is their London postcode (Alison's own 'hood' SW11), at some point their lives intriguingly and fleetingly touch each other.

The subtitle of the piece is 'Four women on the verge of a nervous breakthrough' (sic) and, as well as displaying virtuosity, they make a statement about how we underestimate the inner lives of characters who seem, at first sight, stereotypical. In one way this is Alison's statement not only about how women are perceived, but how women are often portrayed in popular drama. The first character, for example, is representative of the sort of person Alison is now asked to play on television.

Peripheral to the storyline, they are typically the wives of bank managers, vicars and colonels, or if a thriller series, their widows. Given the stage to herself, an ambassador's wife, Claire, reveals an inner life full of pain, complexity and ultimately hope. Alison is giving voice to the under-parted.

Though in strong contrast, the following three creations – an Italian café owner's wife, a new-age alternative healer, and a feisty businesswoman – each take the audience by surprise with the trajectory of their lives and the unpredictability of their personalities. Working with her director Jeremy Stockwell, an expert on physical theatre, the women are distinguished by very individual body language and vocal delivery. There is no need of elaborate costume changes and the few accessories used are changed within sight of the audience. Most importantly, Alison acknowledges, is what each woman wears on her feet. Like the late Dame Edith Evans she only feels her characters are complete when she gets the shoes right.

Originally written to prove to herself that she could write good monologues, Alison needed persuading to take the next step and present the pieces publicly. She admits that this reticence was partly the fear of failure, but after a gentle launch to an audience of friends she realised the potential. Without an iconic subject matter, or a household name on stage, it hasn't proved easy to promote the show, but following a successful showing in Edinburgh and a notable return to Scarborough, the play has built a reputation, and a booking agency now spares Alison the pain of self-promotion. The veteran critic Irving Wardle declared *Are There More of You?*, 'the most thrilling one-woman show I've seen since Ruth Draper'.

5. A Play Revisiting a Fictional Creation

Literature sets plenty of precedents for taking a character from fiction and using their perspective to offer new insights into the original. Jean Rhys's *Wide Sargasso Sea* reveals the first Mrs Rochester from *Jane Eyre*, and Auden's poem 'The Sea and the Mirror' gives us, in 'Caliban to the Audience', his perspective on Shakespeare's savage from *The Tempest*. Most famously in modern drama, Tom Stoppard's first major play, *Rosencrantz and Guildenstern are Dead*, gives us an existential viewpoint of *Hamlet* from two of Shakespeare's least rewarding characters.

Taking a character out of context is an intriguing challenge, but also fraught. Audiences who know the original source material may be tolerant of your speculation, even of your fantasising a little, but you cannot afford to make factual errors in your retelling any more than in a biographical play about a real person. Part of the challenge, and much of the fun in the revisionist approach, is keeping faith with the provenance of your story, so be totally conversant with the wellspring of your tale, and have a convincing justification for every liberty you may take.

Major or minor?

Will you tell your story through the leading character from the original narrative or a secondary one? A major character will already have been fully fleshed out by its creator, so you will have firm guidelines to recreate their physical appearance and personality. Using the conduit of a minor character or characters to explore your principal subject and their narrative offers you more scope for invention, and a chance to offer different perspectives.

Will you choose to revisit your fictional figure in a wholly original script, or co-opt the character's creator as a co-writer? Having an established novelist or playwright to plunder for your show will give you access to great literary material, though it can be intimidating for whoever is writing the rest of your script.

You may also choose to separate the fictional character or characters from their original context and use them to inhabit a wholly new narrative.

CASE STUDY

Roger Llewellyn, *Sherlock Holmes*

Roger Llewellyn was playing Sherlock Holmes in an adaptation of *The Hound of the Baskervilles* in Stoke-on-Trent, where a Holmes expert, David Stuart Davies, saw and admired his performance. They met after the show and Roger posited the idea of a solo show on the great detective. Though a prolific and successful author, Stuart Davies had never written a play and at first dismissed the idea of writing Holmes without his companion, and the chronicler of his adventures, Dr Watson. His inspiration came when he imagined an older Holmes returning to 221b Baker Street on the day of Watson's funeral, recalling their adventures together, and adding fictional biographical material to enhance Conan Doyle's own fictional creation. Holmes, having always been reported by his amanuensis, here has his own voice to narrate and recreate the drama of his early career. As Holmes in the Conan Doyle stories is an unmatchable impersonator there is plenty of scope too for multiple characterisations, from arch villains and ploddish policemen to Mrs Hudson, the famous pair's housekeeper.

Roger asked me to direct *Sherlock Holmes – The Last Act*, and as an Artistic Associate with the Salisbury Playhouse I was able to approach the theatre and suggest premiering in the same space where my play *Shylock* had opened a couple of years before. Two Salisbury Playhouse patrons who, in the role of 'angels', donated extra funding, added to the theatre's input, and we played for a week in the studio theatre, later taking the show to Edinburgh. There the play aroused sufficient critical and public interest to achieve that rarest of Edinburgh feats by more than covering its costs.

The creative team of an inexperienced playwright, an actor new to solo performing and a director with only limited interest in the play's subject might seem unpromising. However, there was a constant and dynamic exchange of knowledge and skills so that we came up with an end product designed not only to appeal to Conan Doyle aficionados but to a larger public who appreciated skilful storytelling, fine acting and were prepared to enter into Holmes's world.

With a head for business and a resolve to make the venture commercially viable, Roger formed his own company and acted as producer – and sole company member. He organised his own print publicity, approached and negotiated with venues, and with sufficient technical experience of lighting and sound dispensed with the need to tour a technician. Only when the number of bookings coming in left him insufficient time to market his own work did he engage a tour booker and relieve himself of the administrative burdens.

When, a decade later, *Sherlock Holmes – The Last Act* began to look as if it was exhausting the supply of suitable venues, the booking agent Mark Makin suggested the original team get together and come up with a second Holmes vehicle for Roger. *Sherlock Holmes – The Death and Life* repeated the success of the first effort, and together the pieces have played over six hundred performances and continue to tour.

6. A Play Celebrating a Literary Life (by impersonation or in recital)

Literary lives

The attraction of writers, poets and playwrights to people who work in and go to the theatre is obvious. Their lives will usually be well documented, often by the writers themselves, and this will be invaluable to your biographical research. If the subject has family, friends or associates still living you have the opportunity to gain new insights by approaching them for recollections or opinions. You will have to decide which biographical details you want to emphasise to tell your version of the truth, and at some point are bound to risk controversy by the exclusion or inclusion of disputed material.

The audience will be there to learn more about a character they know primarily through the written word, so decide if you want to include some of their literary output in your piece. If they are still in copyright you will need to submit your script to their representative and pay the appropriate royalty for the amount of their work you have included.

The inconsistencies in a writer's life are often what intrigues, as much as the narrative. Writers, compassionate on the page, could be tyrannical in their everyday lives. The fluency of the subject's writing can contrast with their lack of verbal or social skills in life to offer an intriguing conjunction. Somerset Maugham, so effortlessly articulate on the page, was rendered incoherent by his crippling stammer.

At what period in his or her life will your subject be telling their story? Is your writer complacent about his fame or self-critical and unfulfilled? It is often showing the minutiae and eccentricities of a literary giant's story that will breathe life into your performance. Their conflicts, rivalries and disappointments are theatrically as interesting as their towering achievements. Don't let your admiration for your subject blind you to his or her fallibility.

The most popular men and women of letters will have been profiled before, and there are multiple takes on the lives of Shakespeare, Wilde, Austen and the Brontës. Choosing a less celebrated figure might narrow the initial appeal of your play, but you will be breaking new ground, which could be to your advantage.

CASE STUDY

John Fraser, *J.M. Barrie – The Man Who Wrote Peter Pan*

John Fraser had no notion of writing and performing a one-man play before he was invited to take a show of his own devising to the Edinburgh Festival. Determined to celebrate the life of a fellow Scot, he first considered profiling his favourite Scottish author, Robert Louis Stevenson. The disparity in their height and girth (Stevenson was tall and thin, neither of which describes John) discouraged him, as did Stevenson's early death at the age of forty-four (John was already in his sixties).

J. M. Barrie was very much a second choice, but a timely book by Andrew Birkin called *The Lost Boys* proved an inspiration. Approaching Birkin for guidance, John, never a particular admirer of Barrie's work beyond *Peter Pan*, became fascinated with this complex man. He learnt of an impotent

---

husband who became besotted with the five young sons of a family he first met when walking in the park, eventually adopting them all after their parents' deaths. Barrie was also one of the richest and most successful authors in the world, earning vast royalties, not just from his plays but also from their adaptations into Hollywood movies.

After four to five months of writing, John took the script to the veteran solo performer, Frank Barrie, (no relation) who admired the research but commented that the piece was not yet a play. A collaboration between the two, based on a professional relationship of decades, resulted in a ninety-minute piece in which James Barrie address the audience directly about his life and work. Towards the end of his life, he talks of his success but also about his very humble origins, his feelings of inadequacy and his enigmatic relationships, particularly with children.

The skill of John's approach is that his subject narrates his story with sincerity and truthfulness, but with sufficient subtext to give the audience the opportunity to reach their own conclusions about his true motives and emotions.

Set simply and elegantly in Barrie's study, there are atmospheric lighting states, some incidental music, and the recorded voices of characters from *Peter Pan*. John was unable to resist a moment of theatrical magic, totally in keeping with the spirit of Barrie's work, when the fairy Tinker Bell makes her ethereal presence felt.

From its premiere at the official Edinburgh Festival, the show was part of John's life, though by no means his sole employment, for half-a-dozen years.

> The show could have had a much longer life, but alongside his other solitary pursuit as a writer, John felt that solo touring didn't suit his naturally gregarious nature and that turning up alone in a remote country town waiting for the technician to arrive and open the venue, before performing and retiring to a lonely B&B for the night was too dispiriting in the end.
>
> As a farewell to the show he accepted an invitation to play it as a platform performance on the stage of the Olivier before the National Theatre's memorable production of *Peter Pan* in 1997.

Paying tribute

Your imagination may have been fired by a literary figure, but rather than impersonate that figure you may choose to reveal them exclusively through their own words. Your show will then be more of a celebration of or tribute to their work.

Shakespeare is surely the most plundered writer of all by solo performers. From Steven Berkoff's *Shakespeare's Villains* to Michael Pennington's *Sweet William* and Susannah York's *The Loves of Shakespeare's Women*, high-profile actors have given us individual insights into the plays. John Gielgud in the middle of the twentieth century, when his career was in a temporary decline, notably performed an anthology of speeches from Shakespeare in his *Ages of Man* programme.

Whilst the upside of adding your contribution to this genre is that the worldwide audience's appetite for such work seems inexhaustible, there is a downside: unless your approach is highly original it will already have been done.

And, like an instrumentalist tackling a difficult concerto, you should only attempt it if you a skilled and experienced Shakespeare performer.

Each of the actors cited above chose their author's extracts to illustrate a theme or support a thesis. Just including your favourite bits from your chosen author and stringing them together with a narration might make a good recital performance but it will lack the sense of purpose and cohesion needed for an evening of theatre. If audiences are very familiar with an author they will appreciate the inclusion of popular works, but equally relish the surprise of less familiar or even unknown pieces. You can flatter their erudition and take them by surprise at the same time.

Charles Dickens famously gave dramatic renditions of his own stories, as well as extracts from his novels, which he toured tirelessly on both sides of the Atlantic, eventually to the detriment of his health. With the author helpfully out of copyright, there was an opening for an actor to pretend to be Dickens and recreate those marathon performances. In 1951, Emlyn Williams grabbed the opportunity during a lull in his own writing and acting career and toured, dressed and made up like Dickens, all over the world for the next thirty years. That baton was taken up by Simon Callow who, also physically impersonating the author, performed a replica programme of one of Dickens' recitals at the 2008 Edinburgh Festival.

This recital approach in character works most effectively when the author is a familiar physical presence, like Dickens. When this isn't the case the actor, as narrator, is a more neutral figure and this frees him or her to recreate the characters within the fiction without using their creator as a conduit. The first one-man show I directed was a collection of short stories by an author, popular but not a popular personality, H. E. Bates, author of *The Darling Buds of May*. The actor, David Neal, had performed them on radio and wanted to expand his characterisations on stage. As the storyteller he introduced us to Bates's collection of Northamptonshire country folk in five bucolic yarns, fusing narrative and characterisation, but very much in David's own skin and not in impersonation of the writer.

CASE STUDY

Miriam Margolyes, *Dickens' Women*

Anthologising writings of the literary greats, with or without biographical reference, is bound to reflect the personal taste of the compiler or performer. Describing Dickens as the 'intellectual centre' of her life, Miriam Margolyes was hooked from the age of ten after reading *Oliver Twist*, and her passion inspired the show.

It was never intended to be a one-woman performance, but a two-hander with an actor playing Dickens and the male characters. Circumstances, including the rejection of a commissioned and paid-for script from an established playwright, as well as the withdrawal of the other player, forced her reluctantly to go solo. But from the beginning Miriam was collaborating with a valued colleague, the director Sonia Fraser, whom she acknowledges as the co-creator of *Dickens' Women*.

Starting offstage with the cries of the wicked and wonderful Mrs Gamp, the piece immediately plunges the audience into Dickens' world, and only when the drunken old lady falls asleep in a chair and it is Miriam Margolyes who awakes to address them as herself do they know the nature of the

---

entertainment – an unashamedly personal take on the author's life and work.

From all the characters she might have impersonated she chooses only those who have some autobiographical significance for Dickens, and will serve her own particular view of the novelist. Her feminist perspective cannot ignore Dickens' obsession with very young women as objects of admiration and desire, and his inability to relate to sexually mature women as reflected in his private life.

In London the show played with a full set and live incidental music, but for touring purposes it was redesigned to need only a lectern, two chairs, a rostrum and a stool for Miriam's embodiment of the dwarf, Miss Mowcher. For all twenty-three characters, including two males, she used only one generic costume with no additional hats, scarves or props, except for a book. The running time was a total of two hours including an interval.

Miriam failed at being her own producer, confused and frustrated by matters relating to tax and insurance, so bookings were handled by her agent and in spite of requests from others to perform the show she resolutely refuses to release the rights in her lifetime. For a very busy and successful actress she believes the impact of the show on her working life has been more psychological than professional. It proved to her that she can indisputably carry a show and this self-confidence has impacted the whole of her subsequent career.

7. A Play Adapted from Other Media

Adapting work from one medium into another has plenty of precedents. Novels in the nineteenth century extended their appeal by being transferred to the stage, and film in the twentieth century was hugely indebted to the theatre. The current West End vogue is for reversing the trend and turning hit films into stage plays and musicals. The one-person show can pilfer from all the above, and more.

Adaptations from other media or shows that anthologise a chosen writer may not require the originality in composition of a brand new story, but be certain that your decision to stage it is more than exchanging your narrative from a written to an aural experience. Radio fulfils that function very well, and axiomatically you can do the ironing whilst engaged in it.

The novel

A well-known novel or novella has the initial appeal of familiarity to an audience and the further advantage of a defined structure to the adapter and performer. With a full-length novel your main constraint will be what to leave out whilst still retaining the integrity of the original. You will probably need to jettison some subplots, peripheral characters and much of the descriptive element, but you have the advantage of your physical presence. Movement, gesture, your face and especially your eyes can be as expressive and communicative as pages of text.

As a guideline on how to truncate the novel and still make sense of the plot it is worth reading a novel and then listening to it as an abridged audio recording and noting the excised passages. Abridged audiobooks are frequently released on two CDs of roughly forty-five minutes each – about the same running time as a full-length solo show.

If the novel's narrator is not a neutral figure but a protagonist and you choose to inhabit his or her voice you don't need to be constrained by the tense in which the author writes. Your stage presentation will benefit from the immediacy of the present.

Faithfully impersonating the physical and psychological characteristics of the novel's protagonists is a great opportunity to show off your versatility, and you will need to practice the art of holding conversations with yourself in different personas. As well as variations in voice and posture the use of a prop or piece of costume such as a hat or scarf can help the audience differentiate your characters with a strong visual clue.

Shorter works of fiction are understandably more popular for adaptation than epics. There are at least half-a-dozen extant one-man versions of Dickens' novella *A Christmas Carol*, including one performed by Patrick Stewart. Several actors have staged Oscar Wilde's *A Picture of Dorian Gray*, and the actor Rodney Bewes successfully tapped into the vein of the comic novel with his versions of George and Weedon Grossmith's *Diary of a Nobody* and Jerome K. Jerome's *Three Men in a Boat*.

Guy Masterson's version of George Orwell's *Animal Farm* adopted the structure of a narrator who guides the audience through the story, introduces the characters and dramatises the action in the present. To differentiate Orwell's collection of assorted pigs, Guy relies on refined physical theatre skills as well as vocal versatility.

The diary

Telling a life story or relating events gleaned from a diary rather than an autobiography has the advantage of demonstrating a more spontaneous response to people and happenings. Even if the diary was written with publication in mind there will be an immediacy that can be lost in a considered recollection, and the writer might reveal vulnerabilities or moments of hubris that would otherwise be edited out. It's a great medium for indiscretion and gossip too, so well suited to the confessional medium of the solo show.

The first one-man show I ever saw was an adaptation from some famous diaries. *Brief Lives* was based on the writings of the seventeenth-century wit and raconteur, John Aubrey, and began life as a half-hour television drama before transferring to the theatre. It was one in a series of short plays on the BBC called *Famous Gossips*. Its author, Patrick Garland, expanded the script for the actor Roy Dotrice who opened in London in 1967 and last performed it in the West End in 2008. When it premiered, the young Dotrice gave a miraculous impersonation of a very old and eccentric man, and during the play's most recent revival he was more than ten years older than Aubrey was at his death. Tenacity, longevity, and a show that waits for you to grow old with it are obviously a winning formula. You should be so lucky.

Patrick Garland had edited the diaries on the premise that the audience is paying a visit to Aubrey who makes up for the absence of friends by recalling them all. This gives the diary extracts a theatrical context, it gives the audience and the player a point of contact, and from the outset a companionable relationship.

In adapting a diary, you or your writer-collaborator will be faced with quite different choices from those offered by other adaptations. Will you use the inherent chronology of the diary, or rearrange it into subjects or separate narratives? Will you decide on a neutral or abstract setting or place your narrator in a definite location like a study or dressing room?

The diary may employ linguistic shortcuts and lack the fluency of conventional literary work so be prepared to take some editorial liberties to make the prose flow in your monologue.

CASE STUDY

Cameron Stewart, *My Grandfather's Great War*

It's the diaries of the famous or notorious, like Anne Frank or Nijinsky, which attract most attention from solo players. Cameron Stewart's piece is based on the First World War exploits of a man who identified himself as 'a very unimportant officer'. But his importance to Cameron is that the officer was his grandfather, who eleven years after the conflict wrote his memoirs in the form of a diary, together with contemporary correspondence that was intended to inform his children and amuse his wife. He had just three copies made, two for his family and one for his regiment.

Realising that their content and literary merit was worthy of much greater exposure, Cameron recorded the diaries as an audio book, was invited to read extracts on BBC Bristol in the days running up to Armistice Day, and was interviewed subsequently on Radio 4's *Today* programme, where 17,000 listeners accessed the website to learn more.

One of the listeners was producer James Seabright, who contacted Cameron to suggest a one-man play, and put him touch with David Benson, a veteran solo player, to collaborate as adapter and director. Having never performed alone on stage, Cameron at first found the rehearsal process uncomfortable, lacking as it did the structure of a conventional play and relying entirely on his resources.

Using Benson's own approach of first addressing the audience as himself, he then quotes dispassionately from the diaries before drawing the audience into the drama of his narrative. Having established an intimate connection, his full-throated enactment of the horrors of trench warfare involves the audience in a very personal and immediate way. The piece ends with Cameron talking to his grandfather about the nature of war, the changing priorities of succeeding generations, and man's relationship with danger and death.

An attachment to his own family history, indignation at the insanity of war, and the opportunity to celebrate a life in the way he knew best are what motivated Cameron to launch his show, and as well as his successful touring there is at last a published record of the diaries, *A Very Unimportant Officer* by Capt. Alexander Stewart, edited by his grandson. Not just a labour of love, insists Cameron, but a labour of love and purpose.

The epic poem

The epic poem seems an obvious target for the solo performer, as that's how the earliest of them would have reached their first illiterate audiences. Homer's *Iliad* was part of the oral tradition at least eight centuries BC.

Only a generation ago Julian Glover tackled the early English epic *Beowulf*, perfectly suited to performance as it is packed with dynamic action. His adaptation even includes some genuine Early English.

To find a poem that is part of an English Literature exam syllabus should generate some audience, and do a service to the poet by breathing life into the verse. There are epic poems by the great stalwarts Byron, Tennyson and Browning but their appeal to a general audience will be limited, and those that claim to be 'dramatic monologues' don't always live up to the promise implied in that title.

Almost certainly intended for reading and not performance is Shakespeare's *The Rape of Lucrece*, but Gerard Logan learned all 1,855 lines and then asked me to direct him in it. I think it is the first time that work, with some judicial cutting, has been performed in this way, and as live theatre it has an entirely new dimension. By characterising the protagonists – rapist, victim and victim's spouse – they take on a much stronger dramatic identity than when the poem is read. The true horror and consequences of the crime of rape are shown in their pain, remorse and fury, which Gerard distinguishes in radically different vocal approaches and body language.

T. S. Eliot's twentieth-century masterpiece *The Waste Land*, as performed by Fiona Shaw and directed by Deborah Warner, had been a success overseas before its first London performances. The collaborative duo were particularly exercised by finding a suitable venue to present this complex and highly charged poem. They chose the bare stage of Wilton's Music Hall in London's East End, a dilapidated old building with, they felt, the perfect atmosphere, setting and acoustic.

CASE STUDY

Linda Marlowe, *'The World's Wife' by Carol Ann Duffy*

As the number of decent parts diminished, the realisation that middle-age was threatening her successful career motivated Linda Marlowe to go solo. Over many years Linda had played the leading female roles in Steven Berkoff's plays and it was he who suggested she anthologise them in a piece called *Berkoff's Women*.

Since the success of that first venture she has staged a new one-woman show every two years, playing the Edinburgh Festival and following up with lengthy and rewarding tours, in the UK and internationally. Her six plays to date could illustrate most of the categories in this selection of solo genres. After that first anthologised work she played a translation of a Spanish one-woman play by Gabriel García Márquez (*Diatribe of Love*), an autobiographical play in the fictional context of the world's oldest wire-walker looking back on an eventful life on the eve of her hundredth birthday (*No Fear*), and a play by Matthew Hurt based on the short stories of Tennessee Williams (*Mortal Ladies Possessed*). Hurt also wrote *Believe* which tells the back stories of four women from the Old Testament, caught up in the wars and conflicts of men.

Carol Ann Duffy's first themed collection of poetry *The World's Wife*, published in 1999, takes stories, histories, characters and myths which focus on men, but presents them from the perspective of the women previously obscured by those men. This feminist approach obviously appealed to Linda, and just as appealing was the dramatic potential in bringing them to life on stage.

Before starting work on the project Linda needed to secure the rights and she approached both Duffy's publisher and her literary agent. With the author's personal permission she was given non-exclusive performing rights for the period of one season, long enough to play Edinburgh and a subsequent tour. The agreement stipulated an advance to be paid on royalties based on ten per cent of the box-office takings or Linda's guaranteed fee, whichever was the greater.

Despite these limited performing rights, Linda went ahead and assembled her creative team. With the producer James Seabright on board, she invited Di Sherlock to collaborate with her as director, and engaged graphic, light and sound designers to ensure her customary high production values.

The World's Wife consists of thirty poems of varying length, so the first task was to choose as many as would fit into the seventy minutes which she aims at for an Edinburgh show. Some, she says, were obvious choices and both the first and last poems functioned as prologue and epilogue to the collection. In the end nineteen women are featured ranging from Mrs Quasimodo to Moors murderer Myra Hindley. The vocal, physical and emotional demands of embodying so many disparate women are what appeals to Linda and what thrills her audience.

After seeing the show, Carol Ann Duffy immediately granted Linda exclusive performing rights to the work for five years.

The full-cast play

The ultimate virtuosic display for a single player is to perform a script written for a full cast. It's one of the rarest manifestations of the solo play but there are successful precedents. Classic plays have been adapted, usually for educational purposes, where the performer, as narrator, guides the audience through the multicharactered scenes, playing both monologue and dialogue to tell the story. As well as vocal and physical virtuosity, this can demand dexterity with props and elements of costume, as well as cross-gender casting.

For a play still in copyright the first obstacle will be to convince the writer or agent that the work will not become a parody of the play, and you would need to present credible reasons for your version. Will it retain the integrity of the original? Will you distort the play's meaning or diminish its characters? Are your motives purely economic or will you bring something original and worthwhile to the production? How much of the play do you intend to cut?

Guy Masterson answered all these questions with his one-man version of Dylan Thomas's *Under Milk Wood*. Originally *A Play for Voices*, Guy, in his uncut version, brings an intense physicality to the characters of the sixty-plus inhabitants of Thomas's fictional village. An effective soundscape, simple lighting changes and minimal costuming concentrates the audience's attention on the poetic language, exactly as the playwright intended.

CASE STUDY

Brian D. Barnes, One Man Theatre

Guy Masterson's feat is matched in daring by a veteran solo performer called Brian D. Barnes who had to correct Guy's assertion that he was the first solo performer to tackle *Under Milk Wood*. Brian had been doing it within a decade of the play's publication in the mid-1960s and it has remained in his repertoire ever since.

As an eager young Australian he had taken ship to Europe to seek out great twentieth-century theatre gurus like Michel Saint-Denis and Helene Weigel, and learn his craft. Whilst in Berlin, Brian gave his first solo performance. After a variety of engagements in England and Australia as director and actor, he decided to devote his life to solo performing and has made that his exclusive employment for over fifty years. He has tackled diaries (*The Incredible Samuel Pepys*), adaptations of classics (*Doctor Faustus*), novels (*Three Men in a Boat*), anthologies (*In the Company of Charles Dickens*), biographies (*The Provocative Oscar Wilde*) and work for children (*The Wind in the Willows*). Most remarkable is his solo version of T. S. Eliot's play *Murder in the Cathedral*.

Originally in a cut version it was one half of an Eliot evening, followed by *Old Possum's Book of Practical Cats* in the second act. Eliot, still alive then, objected to his play being cut and refused performing rights. Relaunching the play, uncut, with Brian playing all the male characters plus the Chorus of the Women of Canterbury, the Eliot estate relented and granted him first the rights to perform in educational establishments, and later worldwide performing rights.

The only concession that Brian makes in this performance of a very dense text is to introduce the enigmatic figures of the four Tempters who visit Thomas Becket by explaining that they represent the exteriorisation of his inner conflict.

Working with a director, Tony Craven, the play is very simply staged with Brian wearing a single robe throughout. *Murder in the Cathedral* runs for ninety minutes and is played without an interval. As well as theatres, the production has always been much in demand in churches and chapels, so the adaptability of the staging has to be matched by Brian's own vocal agility in spaces with notoriously awkward acoustics.

When one German venue approached Brian to perform this play he was surprised, as it seemed very out of character with their usual choice of repertoire. Just before committing himself to do the performance he realised that they were expecting not Eliot's *Murder in the Cathedral* but Agatha Christie's *Murder at the Vicarage*.

You've probably never heard of Brian D. Barnes, but he has an astonishing worldwide following. Touring as 'One Man Theatre' he has played over fifteen hundred shows in eighty-seven countries; that's more than a quarter of all the sovereign states in the world. In 2004, between engagements in Europe, Brian popped home to collect an MBE at Buckingham Palace for his services to drama. The one-man theatre has royal approval.

8. A Play for Children

Solo performances from companies and individuals specialising in theatre for children tap into the oldest and most universal tradition of storytelling. But unlike theatre for adults, which generally embraces audiences from sixteen to senility, their audience has a variable age demographic that is more specifically targeted.

The age groups divide roughly as follows: children aged between eighteen months and three years, between three and five years, then from six to twelve, and teenagers have a category of their own. Less restrictively when playing public theatres, plays are also marketed in categories suitable for a certain age and above.

Shows can range from stories narrated in a classroom to more ambitious stagings in school halls, small-scale venues and studio theatres. For one-off school performances the technical demands are, by necessity, minimal, so the performer will usually travel alone with whatever costumes, props and equipment are required. But lack of elaborate staging and lighting doesn't mean the work cannot be visually exciting and inventive. The use of puppets, objects and music enhances the single acting presence and the ingenuity of the player is matched by the youthful imagination of the audience. Many of the shows invite a high degree of participation from the children that increases their confidence and encourages creativity.

If you have experience of performing to children you will know about their attention span, the humour that appeals to them and the spontaneity of their responses. Pitching your work at the right level for the appropriate age group is crucial, and you will be aware of the dangers of underestimating children's abilities and critical faculties. A one-man play based on *Hamlet*, where a detective follows clues to tell the play's narrative is very successful with its target audience, aged from eight to twelve years old. Arts Council England, who you might approach for funding your project, specifies theatre for young people and children as one of its four priorities.

For those of us who don't want or dare not have these close encounters with this most demanding sector we should be grateful that someone is recruiting future audiences for theatre at an importantly impressionable age.

CASE STUDY

Chris Connaughton, Intext Performance

As well being the company's director, Chris is also the principal performer in a very comprehensive range of programmes for children of all ages. From a 20–35-minute storytelling session for pupils at the Foundation Stage he also offers classic fairytales that usually last between ten or twenty minutes longer, and plays based on literary characters that can last up to an hour. These running times are flexible to suit the school's requirements and any of his repertoire can be performed as part of a full-day or half-day visit, which also includes workshops and related classroom work.

Chris gives guidance on the appropriate size of his audiences, preferring to restrict their numbers to between 100–120, roughly four classes, and encourages parents and carers to attend the performances too, as the stories are often an experience that children want to share, offering speaking and listening opportunities amongst families at home.

A knowledge of how schools function, the structure of the curriculum, and thirteen years' experience of entertaining youngsters in over two thousand schools means Chris really understands his market. He has a set scale of performing fees, and to prepare his young audiences and their teachers he sends out teachers' notes in advance. He also reassures the establishments he visits that he has the appropriate Public Liability Insurance and CRB certificate to enable him to work with minors.

Whilst classifying his work as small-scale in terms of production values, Chris aims that in terms of ideas, language and themes it is anything but. Even though the shows are age-specific he tries to include elements that are a year above what the children might usually be presented with. Children, he insists, know when they are being patronised and hate it as much as adults do. This doesn't only make good artistic and educational sense; it is good for business too.

Chris gains more repeat bookings from being challenging than he loses from being too complicated. As with any piece of theatre, you must respect your audience.

9. A Play Based on Utilising a Special Skill

There are successful one-person shows based not on biography or fiction, but on the special knowledge or skill of the performer. Though this is a less exposing format than the autobiographical approach, you will still need to be comfortable about confronting an audience in your own skin and have the conviction that the subject matter is interesting and accessible enough to hold your audience. You must find a structure that distinguishes your show from a lecture or demonstration. Start with the assumption that your audience does not necessarily share your enthusiasm and needs to be persuaded or wooed into spending time in your company to find out more.

The more unusual your skill, the greater should be its appeal. But you are unlikely to rival the Frenchman Joseph Pujol who performed a solo act over a hundred years ago using his special skill as a flatulist, or farter. By the beginning of the twentieth century, under his professional name of 'Le Pétomane', he had refined his demonstration into a show where he recited a poem, written by himself, using his special skill to imitate the farm animals. So as not to disappoint his audience the show climaxed with his famous impression of the 1906 San Francisco earthquake.

Your vocal virtuosity is a more likely genesis for a show, or your skill with a musical instrument. His neglected skill on the French horn inspired the actor Jonathan Guy Lewis to approach author Jasper Rees after hearing a serialisation of his book *I Found My Horn* on the radio. Picking up a long forgotten skill and attempting to play Mozart's Third Horn

Concerto in E flat, K447 on what the *Guinness Book of Records* calls 'the most difficult instrument in the orchestra' is the challenge that author and performer set themselves, and the play celebrates the journey from aspiration to fulfilment.

If you are sharing your knowledge of a subject with your audience, too much data is deadly. You will want to tell them all you know about your theme, but bombarding them with facts is more likely to alienate than convert them. They will sooner be engaged by the offbeat and the humorous than the purely informative.

Julian Curry is a wine expert as well as an actor, and combined those two talents in a show called *Hic!*, (full title: *Hic – or The Entire History of Wine [abridged]*) aimed at fellow aficionados and those of us who just like a drink. As well as the history of wine, and his own appreciation of it, he teases the audience throughout about the provenance of one particular bottle, which is his principal prop, and he has another full decanter which quenches his thirst during the show. Intriguingly he never divulges the contents of the decanter.

CASE STUDY

Rosemary Hawthorne, *The Knicker Lady*

It was a combination of expertise and financial necessity that launched Rosemary Hawthorne's one-woman show *The Knicker Lady*.

Even as a RADA student Rosemary was fascinated by costume history, and after suspending her acting career to marry and raise seven children she wrote her first book, *Knickers: An Intimate Appraisal* in 1991. Its success proved what a fascination there is amongst the British public in the history and design of ladies' undergarments. Giving illustrated talks to clubs and institutes with the aid of her extensive collection of drawers and bloomers, she realised that there might be a wider public out there.

Rosemary wrote her own script, engaged a director and was contracted to a booking agency to find her engagements. As that contract concluded she and her retired clergyman husband realised that working as a highly motivated pair they could improve on their current success rate and generate a badly needed income.

Fortuitously, before finding his vocation, husband John had been an advertising executive, and scraping together a budget of £5,000 he took responsibility for marketing, publicity and booking the show under the name of Vicarage Productions. The only major element they needed to outsource was a professional web designer for their site which both acknowledge as a vital and invaluable aid.

The co-stars of the show are the dozens of intriguing pantaloons, pantalettes, bras and divided drawers which cram into their large MPV vehicle driven by John, who also liaises with the technical staff at each venue and organises the get-out while Rosemary meets her public and maximises the merchandising potential of her books. The show, with its original music on CD, can be run by one technician handling both lights and sound.

From its original sixty-minute running time the show has now expanded to eighty minutes plus a twenty-minute interval so that conventional venues can benefit from bar takings. But to accommodate the presenter, *The Knicker Lady* remains flexible in terms of content and length. By keeping everything 'in-house' the couple are in complete control of their working output as well as their related finances and currently average forty shows per year, as well as talks and events.

Rosemary is now working on a book about the history of sanitary towels, but is dubious about its potential as her second one-woman show.

10. A Play Based on None of the Above

The idea for your solo show may not conform to any of the examples considered so far. Speech need not be the only or even the primary component of your work; the mix of text and song is a popular variant. Celebrity exponents like Elaine Stritch will illustrate their life stories with songs from the shows that made them famous, and the same strategy has proved very effective in biographical solo plays about Maria Callas, Edith Piaf and Judy Garland.

Marcel Marceau, the celebrated French mime artist, spent his long solo career without uttering a word, performing mimodramas, most famously in his incarnation as Bip the white-faced clown. One of his students, Nola Rae, continues that wordless tradition in this country and around the globe, touring solo plays that explore the comic potential in tragic scenarios. The obvious advantage of excising language from your performance is that every culture will understand you, and the whole world is your potential audience.

From a dance background, Nigel Charnock, a founder of DV8, fuses not just movement and song but includes improvised monologue in his solo work. He breaks down the boundaries of all these performance disciplines to create his maverick shows.

Whatever you choose as the source for your play, keep in mind that experiencing theatre requires all your senses, and all your attention so don't short-change your audience with something they could have read in bed or listened to in the car.

It's crucial to go and see as many solo shows as you can sniff out. You'll have some hideous evenings when you'll lose the will to live almost as soon as the lights go down, but you will learn so much from watching a badly conceived, shoddily written, poorly performed solo show. Go and see them all, good, bad or indifferent, whenever you get the opportunity. Occasionally there'll be an event where the play and the player grab you and hold onto you in a revelatory embrace and you'll remember why you want to go and do likewise.

Finally, the First Word

There are enough imponderables ahead so give yourself something tangible to hang on to – a title for your play. You'll have no dilemma if yours is an adaptation of a book, but if your piece is autobiographical and you're not a household name, your choice will be harder. Peter Searles, who featured here earlier with his very successful trio of traveller's tales, *Hey Gringo*, admits that the title of his hilarious follow-up, *Sex with Peter Searles*, may have inhibited bookings from nervous programmers in the shires. You'll want a title that is catchy, memorable and pertinent but that doesn't frighten the horses. You should practise saying it as well as reading it. What drags them in off the street at the Edinburgh Festival Fringe may not go down so well in rural North Wales or Cheltenham. An audience member booking by phone can be put off by having to articulate a title they find embarrassing.

Biographical plays should of course name the subject in the title or subtitle, but a hint or hook will encourage those who don't necessarily know much about him or her. John Fraser helpfully called his play about J.M. Barrie *The Man Who Wrote Peter Pan*.

Unless you're deliberately targeting a coterie audience, don't make your title an in-joke or obscure literary reference. It will be lost on most of us, and more will feel excluded by not getting it than flattered by being in the know. You want to intrigue, but not to baffle.

PART TWO

Getting Your Act Together

Now you have an idea, if only in outline, of what your show will be, it is time to put your performer's hat to one side for the moment and address some practical issues. We actors are used to working to other people's deadlines; the casting director will give us a cut-off date for accepting or refusing a job, the director will tell us by what date he wants us on stage without a script, and the theatre management will determine when the show opens and closes. These are matters over which an actor rarely has control. Control has now passed to you, and since, even for an actor, time is money you have to learn the discipline of setting your own parameters, and establishing and sticking to deadlines. Here are some broad deadlines you will need to set, not in strict order, to help focus your mind:

1 The date for the first draft of your script
2 The date for your finalised script
3 The date when you will have sufficient funds to start work
4 The date when all your creative team will be in place
5 The dates when rehearsals will begin and end
6 The date of a first, albeit tentative, showing
7 The date when your performance venue will be confirmed
8 The date of your first public performance

In between these rough deadlines will be dozens of others that you will set (and maybe miss), but without a similar list the gestation period can be so drawn out that you may lose your impetus and join that long list of almost-solo players who once had a great idea for a show and never quite got it together. You will discover how committed you are to mounting your play when you confront the distractions and temptations to postpone it.

Money

Your show is going nowhere without money, so you have to address the unavoidable question of financing your project. If you have funds, foresight and business acumen this will be less of a problem for you than to the rest of us. You can see what costs might be involved from this sample list of the people and components that may make demands on your budget before your show has even had its first performance and earned its first fee. Some may not be relevant to you but there will almost certainly be an item here that will take you by surprise.

- Writer
- Director
- Composer/Choreographer/Special skills
- Performer (You!) – rehearsal fees/expenses
- Technical manager/Stage manager
- Rehearsal space
- Technical/dress rehearsal space
- Photoshoot
- Poster and flyer design
- Publicity print
- Website design and hosting
- Travel
- Accommodation

The dream ticket

The ideal scenario would be an invitation to perform at a venue that absorbs all the preparation and production costs, provides rehearsal space, technical resources and personnel, publicises the show and pays you. Some or all of these elements might be provided by a theatre where you have worked or are currently working, and that wishes to encourage your enterprise and talent. Your contribution would fulfil some of the theatre's commitment to new work, and might give the venue access to money from its funding bodies.

An attractive alternative would be finding a producer who has sufficient faith in the project to underwrite the expenses and pay you. If you don't already have a working relationship with or access to any producers you should visit www.theactingwebsite.com and scan the list of UK producers from their very useful database. The site gives you links to the producers' websites where you can see the sort of work they support. Major producers will be unlikely to take an interest in a solo show unless there is a major 'name' attached to it, but there are smaller producers that you can approach. Look at the top of any publicity for solo work to find the producer credited.

The perils of partnership

Although being produced by a theatre or individual producer can ease your financial headaches, you need to reassure yourself about who has artistic control of the production during and after its initial staging. Be clear about how percentages of any future income from your show will be divided, and how each party will be credited. There will be a contract or at least a letter of agreement and, as in all contractual dealings, the devil is in the detail. Don't sign until you are satisfied about exactly what you are sharing, and for how long.

A co-production where you split the costs and take responsibility for an agreed proportion will require the same vigilance.

Public money

You may need to raise all or some of the finance yourself. This has always been an onerous task and fraught with bureaucratic pitfalls, but since the cuts in arts funding of recent times it has become even harder to access funding from public bodies. The pot has got smaller, and the servings have shrunk in proportion.

Start by approaching your local council, which is likely to have an Arts Officer who can advise you on where to access public funding and who you should be getting in touch with. Your regional arts council as well the national organisations can be approached for seed funding for a project they approve. An educational element to your work might appeal to relevant local-government bodies, and if your piece deals with a social issue – say domestic abuse or migrant workers – you might find European Union cash to support you.

For details about Grants for the Arts, including how to apply and the aims of the scheme, see the Arts Council England website at www.artscouncil.org.uk. (Other websites for funding bodies are listed in the Appendix.)

Corporate sponsorship

Sponsorship from firms and companies is another source of funding, but also needs a targeted approach. Companies get so many requests that you should only appeal to those who will get something out of forming a relationship with you and some value from supporting your work. For example, the Wellcome Trust takes an interest in scientific or medical themes, and the Goethe Institute has a reputation for subsidising work that promotes German culture. The organisation Arts and Business is set up to spark new partnerships between commerce and culture, and their website (www.artsandbusiness.org.uk) will give you details of their brief. There is also a facility to search for information on funding on the National Lottery website (www.lotteryfunding.org.uk).

By scanning theatre brochures and leaflets you will get a helpful indication of those institutions regularly associated with the arts. Recognition and their logo on your print publicity will be the least expected in return, and you may be able to offer them an advert in your programme or even a front-of-house display.

Trusts and foundations

There are many charitable trusts that fund arts projects, amongst the highest-profile ones being:

- The Calouste Gulbenkian Foundation
- The Esmee Fairbairn Foundation
- The Peter De Haan Charitable Trust
- The Clore Duffield Foundation
- The Paul Hamlyn Foundation
- The Oxford Samuel Beckett Theatre Trust

Their contact details can be found in the Appendix, and a more comprehensive list is available using the website for the Association of Charitable Foundations (www.acf.org.uk). Before applying for funding be scrupulous about whether your project meets their remit so that you won't be wasting your time or theirs.

Before making approaches to funding bodies or potential sponsors on your own behalf you should have an information pack prepared, explaining why you need and deserve their financial or practical support. This should have a summary of your project, details of the personnel involved, images where available and some sort of mission statement.

People

Working with other actors is one of the pleasures of our profession. We speak the same language, whinge about the same things, laugh at the same in-jokes. Some of us refer to non-actors as 'civilians', as though we were perpetually on the front line; taking risks, special, unappreciated, but having more fun than anyone else. Well, now you are on a dangerous solo mission and whether you come back with a medal or with a fatal wound to the ego, you will have done it without a comrade to nudge or bitch with. And on the way you will have encountered a lot of people who don't think that acting is the only thing worth doing with a life.

There must be solo shows where the performer has wowed audiences in an entertainment crafted entirely without help from a second, third or fourth party. But they will be the exceptions. You will have had dealings with some of these creative people in other circumstances, but your relationships will be very different when you are the only player and possibly the producer too. Your collaborators will most likely be one of the following:

Playwright

If you are not writing or devising your show, finding and commissioning a playwright to write your script is obviously the most significant choice you will make at the start of your working process. You will need to be clear how much control you want before and during the writing period, and make sure that your writer understands the level of involvement you require and is agreeable to it. Many playwrights are used to collaborative work in companies that specialise in new writing, but some expect a high level of autonomy and would not respond well to excessive input beyond the initial stages.

Without a writer you have worked with before you will need to approach one whose work you admire, or who has been recommended to you. In such a new relationship you should have exploratory meetings to assure each other that the partnership can work and that you are on the same wavelength. Internet searches, playwrights' agents and *The Writers' and Artists' Yearbook* can all help you locate writers and a search of Doollee.com will alert you to those who are experienced in writing for one player.

Uniquely in this instance the playwright is there to serve you, rather than the other way round, so be aware of that dynamic and don't commit yourself to it unless you are reasonably confident it will bring credit to you both. Ask for some pages of a sample script to see whether you are on the same wavelength and that the writer's style will suit your vision of the play.

You are both professionals and your average writer is as likely to be underemployed and underpaid as your average actor, so be realistic about the cost of rewarding their input and be clear from the outset what the financial arrangements will be. Consult the guidelines as laid down by the Writers' Guild (see the Appendix).

PROFILE

Stewart Permutt, playwright

Stewart Permutt is a published playwright with strong credentials as a writer of monologues. When approached to write a solo play he believes both parties must have valid artistic motives for establishing a working relationship, and he certainly would not respond to an invitation from an actor simply looking for a vehicle to display their talents, or one where Stewart's only incentive was his fee. The actor should also know that the character to Stewart is more important than the player. He also maintains that although a twenty-minute monologue can be sustained as pure character study, a seventy-minute or full-length piece needs action. Action in this instance means actable material, something beyond an exploration of personality. He also prefers to use the present tense and not the recollected past to reveal this action.

His most successful solo play started life as a twenty-minute monologue in an evening of four such pieces called *Singular People*, which played at Edinburgh and the London fringe. A management asked him to develop one of the women's stories into a longer play using the same character but with a different theme. After an initial resistance he realised that the protagonist and the plot could both benefit from these changes of treatment and the rewritten play became *Unsuspecting Susan*. Although not written with her in mind, Celia Imrie played the part of Susan and the full-length play had great success in the UK and America. It is published in a volume of one-woman plays called *Singular (Female) Voices* along with work by playwrights

Anna Reynolds, Moira Buffini and Catherine Johnson.

Stewart's pragmatic professionalism shows how a collaboration can work, but he is realistic about when that collaboration becomes too much of a compromise and the partnership is unworkable. He has parted with actors, sometimes amicably and sometimes not, at various stages in the creative process when there are irreconcilable differences. To minimise the stress and potential expense of such breakdowns, Stewart works within the guidelines established by the Writers' Guild.

Director

It's a mistake to think that the scale and intimacy of a solo show means you can dispense with a director. An outside eye is essential, not just for coordinating the practical elements of the performance, but to ensure at the very least the clarity of the text, variety of the delivery and the tone of the performance. We all need to be told if we're being inaudible, too slow or too self-indulgent. A good director will bring a great deal more in terms of artistic choices and give you a confidence that you would lack by going it alone.

The stage at which a director becomes involved in your work will vary from case to case. (The idea for your show may well have come from a director so you will be in partnership from the beginning, probably collaborating on the script if you are writing your own show.) If engaging a writer you might wish to have a director on board at the commissioning stage to work with you and the playwright as a triumvirate. You may choose to wait for a late or final draft of the script before approaching someone to oversee the production.

As a working actor you will have experience of different directors, and can approach someone with whom you are confident of a fruitful relationship. If no one leaps to mind, or your chosen director is unavailable, you can consult fellow actors about their experiences. Ideally you should also see the director's work and, before committing yourself, meet to discuss your individual approaches to the play and the process. An actor choosing a director is usually an option open only to stars, but don't be intimidated by the reversal of roles.

Like writers familiar with creating monologue, there are directors used to working on a one-to-one basis with an actor. They will know it is a much more intense and demanding relationship than working with a member of a cast, and that there should be a level of equality not always present in rehearsal situations. You will need to be sensitive to each other's energy levels, and adapt your working pace and schedule appropriately.

The rate at which your director is paid will depend on the level of his or her contribution. Much of the preparation for a full-cast play will not apply to your work, and the rehearsal period will probably be shorter. Under the auspices of a theatre or a producer you may not have to concern yourself with fees, but if negotiating with the director or their agent yourself you should try and make the financial arrangements as uncomplicated as possible. Residual payments or royalties to the director can make a small-scale enterprise unnecessarily complicated, and a one-off fee *might* be acceptable to all parties. Ask the director what fee he or she would be prepared to accept for the preparation work and rehearsal of your play, and negotiate from there. In some instances you may need to consider a percentage payment or a fixed-sum per performance to secure the director's services.

Designer/Lighting designer

A single chair and adequate illumination have been the only design elements in so many successful solo shows. At the other extreme that seminal production of *Brief Lives* with Roy Dotrice featured a hugely elaborate and brilliant set by Julia Trevelyan Oman, boasting hundreds of props, many of them genuine antiques.

If you are opting for somewhere in between, the input of a set and costume designer and a lighting designer can add useful dimensions to your show. With only you to look at, some extra visual stimulus will be a bonus, and changes in lighting can helpfully establish different locations and moods. You and/or your director can decide on the scale of their contribution and approach designers experienced in small-scale work for limited budgets. They should appreciate that a conventional designer's contract and remuneration are not applicable, and you can negotiate an equitable hourly or daily rate for the time they devote to your project.

Remember that if you are planning to tour your show you will want to minimise the extra physical elements you have to transport. Similarly, if your lighting plot is overelaborate and dependant on special effects, you are adding to your problems when you get-in at venues and possibly incurring extra equipment costs.

You will probably conclude that aiming for simplicity is not just a sound artistic conclusion, but a wise financial one too.

Composer/Choreographer/Special skills

Incidental music can enhance your work as much as design and lighting, and there may be movement sequences in your play that require special tuition. If using pre-recorded music a royalty must be paid and this is administered by the PRS (Performing Right Society). You can find out about them at www.prsformusic.com. You will need to complete a PRS return listing the music you use, the original artists who created it, and the duration of the extracts. The fee payable will normally be covered by your venue's rolling PRS licence, though occasionally you may be responsible for a proportion of it.

If commissioning original music or a sound design for your show, you will need to negotiate fees with the composer and/or sound designer in the same way as you did for the designer and lighting designer, though if royalties are involved, as with a writer, you can refer to the PRS.

To find a choreographer and find out the relevant payment structure visit www.danceuk.org.

Like everyone in a creative team you should agree in advance where and how they will be credited in your print publicity.

Stage manager

Though it is possible, and certainly more economical, to rely on the technical staff of the venue where you are playing, many solo actors prefer to play and tour with their own stage manager. Unless you are very confident of the technical aspects of theatre, or have minimal technical requirements, you would be wiser doing so.

A conventional production would have a stage-management presence from the start or even before the start of rehearsals, and this would be a team rather than an individual. It is most likely and more cost-effective that you would involve a single stage manager for a solo show at a later stage, possibly the last week of rehearsals, where his or her contribution to the running of the show becomes essential.

You would need to be confident that your stage manager has all the skills necessary to run, call and very probably operate your show. If you're not lucky enough to know such an individual you should contact colleagues and theatres where you have worked to ask for a recommendation. There is also a very useful website (www.uk.stagejobspro.com) that can direct you to someone suitably qualified, but you should certainly meet the individual before committing yourself to employing them. Your reliance on that person will be enormous – and compatibility is vital. During a run or on tour, your stage manager will almost certainly be the person you see and spend most time with.

If you are employing the stage manager on a weekly basis you should consult Equity (www.equity.org.uk) to find the current minimum wage to base your offer on, or negotiate a daily rate if your schedule is more sporadic.

Unpaid help

Each of the professionals listed above will want your work to succeed, but it's important for your morale that you acquire a separate support network of people who will encourage you without being on your payroll.

In the first instance it may be a friend, family member or colleague who has spurred you on to go it alone. They will have seen the pluses that attracted you to this format in the first place: autonomy, empowerment, control, fulfilment, achievement. Others will be less supportive and draw your attention to what you should already know are the minuses: very hard work, responsibility, liability, isolation, possibly failure. Go with the positive-thinkers, share your concerns with them and don't take your inevitable doubts to the other camp who will be waiting to say 'I told you so.'

Whether you are working with a finished script, a work in progress, or just a few notes on the back of an envelope, you need someone to bounce your ideas off. This should be someone in addition to your writer, if you are collaborating with one, as he or she has almost as much at stake as you. It must be someone whose artistic sensibility you trust, but not someone who will only offer you reassurance.

The best one-person shows I have experienced as a practitioner and as an audience have nearly all had the input of a director, but if you feel you do not need one, cannot afford to pay one, or don't know one you trust sufficiently, then this honest and realistic collaborator is all-important. Test out your concept, your narrative, your voice. Is the premise of your show appealing, is its trajectory clear, and does it satisfy the criteria of a good evening in the theatre?

If you have written your own script then your ally becomes indispensible. After all the work you have put in, you will want to use all your research, demonstrate all your knowledge, display all your skills. These may be genuine achievements, but will they contribute to the purpose of your play and the enjoyment of your audience? A shrewd, impartial eye will tell you whether you are making good theatre or just showing off.

With as many or as few colleagues as you have chosen to collaborate with, and your support network in place, you can start work in earnest.

Timing

Defining the scale of your play will be one of your first challenges. There are precedents for solo shows that last anywhere between a frisky half-hour and a bum-numbing three hours or longer. The strength of your subject matter, your stamina, and the stamina of your target audience will concentrate the mind when making that decision, and it is more likely that your show will contract rather than grow in length.

Even with full-cast plays, more and more are now performed without interval, running anywhere between seventy and one hundred minutes. At the Edinburgh Festival Fringe most solo plays run between fifty and seventy minutes, and some venues stipulate an hour as maximum.

When touring, many venue managers will request an interval during the programme as it's a way to enhance their income with bar sales, another reason to be flexible about the structure of your show when possible. When marketing your play it is often useful to offer the option of a full-length and a truncated version to suit the venue's requirements, assuming that doesn't make too many artistic compromises.

Under your belt

The second question that most 'civilians' ask actors (after 'Would I have seen you in anything?') is usually, 'How do you learn the lines?' With solo players that unanswerable question often gets promoted to first place. And it is a huge hurdle to jump. Even if you have played major roles in long plays, or shared the burden in a two-hander, you will now be facing a very different challenge. It's not just the sheer volume of words that you must memorise, but that with no other performer on stage, you will get no prompts to provoke your vocal or emotional reactions or to move the story forward. There is also nobody to help you get back on track if things go wrong.

Many playwrights are insistent that you observe their punctuation, and sometimes this aids the learning process; a full stop or a paragraph break will be the right impetus to start a new thought or provoke a change of energy. When this isn't the case you should feel freer to impose your own rhythms by changing these linguistic signals to suit your own mental and emotional journey. Reformat the script if necessary, as the memory of the gap between paragraphs, or a page ending, can become an indelible stumbling block to your progress. This might be a cavalier approach to dialogue but in a monologue you are solely responsible for the truth of what you say.

Find mental markers in your script as aides-memoires. Highlight them if it helps. They don't need to be logical changes of thought or direction, but associate that word or phrase with a change of mood, a physical movement or an alteration in pace, and you can build up a series of signposts that will guide you through the least linear text and get you off the book with a sense of security.

Rehearsals

Will you start rehearsals with your script wholly or part learnt, or do you intend to absorb your lines during the working period? Some directors advocate a thorough command of the text before day one, and others prefer the flexibility of a fluid approach. Reach a consensus with your director on which working method you adopt to forestall frustration in the early stages of rehearsal.

You'd be at an obvious advantage if you have written your own script, or if the development process is over a very long period. Whatever the rehearsal period, if you are working together with a writer and director on a new play it's likely that the script will be changing along the way. This is a wonderfully organic way to produce good work, but at some point someone will need to put a halt to the rewriting and finalise the script. You will know that unlearning lines and substituting new ones can be very arduous and it will probably need to be you that sets a deadline for rewrites because it is your sole responsibility to be secure in your lines before the first performance.

When collaborating with a director, the time you spend on 'table' work, forensic exploration of the script, will, of course, depend on the density of the text and your individual approaches to the work process. It's a good way to ease yourself into rehearsal, and postpones the true terror of getting up there all by yourself. Try and find a neutral but congenial space for this, but not one so cosy that the distractions of phones, visitors or children are inescapable.

Rehearsal space

You will need to move in to a larger space in the later stages of rehearsal which should at least represent the size of your projected playing area and where the director is not too intimidatingly close. Dedicated rehearsal spaces can be very expensive, but multipurpose church halls or community centres will offer more acceptable hourly rates, and function rooms in pubs are often willing to rent out the space out of opening hours.

Rehearsing in the space

The dynamics of rehearsing a solo show, you will find, are radically different from those of preparing a conventional play. The intensity of the work will strain your mental concentration, your physical stamina and your creative energy. In my experience, after four hours' work, even with scheduled breaks, both player and director can start to lose their edge. Don't be ashamed to say when your brain starts to hurt and you need to stop, absorb and recharge before the next session.

If you have an extended creative team – a designer, lighting designer, choreographer or composer, for example – let them share your progress as soon as you feel comfortable. With only two of you working away, the process risks becoming insular and it's a release to have other interested parties there to broaden your focus. They will also be able to tune in to the style of the performance and that will inform their contribution.

With a performance venue and date in your diary for the opening of your show, the pressures will at least be quantifiable. You can have the usual run-throughs, technical and dress rehearsals, maybe even the luxury of a free preview or two, before facing your first paying audience. Rehearsing your show in anticipation of finding somewhere to do it removes those deadlines, but it will prolong the stress and encourage procrastination. Fix a date for a showing, however modest and however imperfect the performance space, to test-drive the piece in front of friends, colleagues and people whose opinions you value. Call it a workshop performance or work-in-progress if that eases the pressure, but do it.

What do you think of it so far?

Feedback is hugely valuable at this stage – as long as it doesn't undermine you. Take very seriously comments on clarity, audibility, consistency of characterisation and factual accuracy, but be wary of more generalised observations on the concept or the interpretation that you and your director have worked so hard to realise.

First Night

However your show is funded, whatever its subject matter and wherever you premiere it, the one constant thing you share with all solo performers is the unique terror you will feel on the opening night. Just comfort yourself with the knowledge that the first performance of your first solo show can only happen once in a lifetime. You can mitigate the dread by packing the show with sympathetic friends, family and fellow artists who will be on your side and willing you to succeed. Just getting through it will be your first major achievement, and whatever goes wrong it can't detract from that remarkable feat.

With the first one under your belt you should try not to leave too long a gap before the next. You may be lucky enough to start with a short run, where over a period of four or five nights you can settle the show in a little, gain confidence in your choices and iron out the problems that will have become evident to you and your director. Too long a period between outings and each show will seem like a slightly less traumatising version of the first.

The morning after the night before

Expect, after the euphoria of performing, that you will wake up next day feeling exhaustion at a level you have never encountered before. Tim Miller, an American actor, says, 'Solo performance demands the stamina and the stick-to-it-iveness of a pit bull terrier running a marathon to turn in a winning lottery ticket.' Of course the effort of remembering the text and your vocal and physical exertions will have tired you, but it's the relentless concentration that will have taken its toll. There is not a moment on that stage when you are not inhabiting your character or characters, playing your audience like a fly-fisherman, keeping that fragile bubble afloat.

You will spend endless hours analysing what went wrong on the first night, or what went right on the first night and wrong on the second. You'll be champing at the bit to get back on stage and try something new, sharpen your focus, and enrich your relationship with the audience. They can smell your fear, so whatever is happening to your heart rate or your bowels, work at making them feel safe in your company. You only have each other.

Just keep doing it

What you need after that first high-wire display is to do it again, and again, as often as you can. Offer to perform it free, for charities, in any space that can accommodate the show and enough people to make it a performance. You will be astonished at how the play and your playing grow and mature between each showing. You will gain confidence in your grasp of the lines, and your journey through the evening.

As an actor in a company you'd use the interval of a show to discuss the audience with your fellows. If you're all getting your laughs, or can sense an appreciative silence, you'll love them, but at a deadly matinee full of humourless bronchitics, you'll feel differently. It's an 'us' and 'them' relationship. When it's just 'you' and 'them', that relationship changes; you are in a minute-by-minute partnership where your every word, move, gesture or raised eyebrow can change the dynamic. That is why performing a solo show, even in a long run, is never dull. You don't have the option to be bored because any slackening of the bond between you and your public is potentially fatal to the success of the show. They will pick up on any lack of commitment from you, and if the show is stale you will fail.

Next Steps

Been there... Done that

Having proved to yourself that you can do it, you may decide to move on. It takes that initial exposure to discover that solo performing is too lonely, too arduous or too badly paid to pursue beyond those first performances. Whether you have had a positive or bruising experience you'll be a different actor when you go back to conventional work, and an enriched one, professionally at least.

A future for your show

If you want to give your show a future life you will need to make some decisions that can affect your working life in the mid- and even the long term. Juggling a jobbing actor's career with a solo one is not as straightforward as it may seem. Many actors toy with the idea of having a show in their back pocket which they can choose to bring out when other work is quiet or they feel like a change. This is attractive but quite unrealistic. Most venues that will book and pay you to appear plan their programmes between six months and a year in advance. You could be committing yourself to a one-off performance so far in the future that you cannot possibly predict what other work might be on offer. Contemplate the reality of having to turn down a great part in a regional theatre, a run in the West End or some lucrative television work to do one show ten months hence for the modest fee that you will command.

A plan

Your strategy should be to devote a period of months or weeks to performing your solo play, and set aside that tranche of time as far in advance as you can. Booking periods are usually defined as spring and autumn seasons, though they span the whole year with gaps for Christmas, when venues cater for that season, or high summer when theatres often go dark. Prime touring months are February to May, and September to the end of November. Making yourself free in July and August, unless you're going to the Edinburgh Fringe or yours is an end-of-the-pier show, is not going to be very productive.

Now that you've created the gap, you have to fill it. With a producer or producing theatre already on board who believes that touring the show can be profitable, you have someone experienced to organise your dates. If they are not interested in further involvement you can find a booking agent or organising the tour yourself. Your contract with the producer should have covered this contingency, but make sure the financial implications are clear to you.

Getting bookings

If you can't find a tour booker to take your show on, or feel you can organise your own dates, you should realise that both promoting and performing your play is very time-consuming and will become your principal employment. You will need to have tenacity, patience and great communication skills. You will have to be numerate, articulate and totally reliable. On many occasions exercising those skills will be called upon to make up for the shortcomings of the personnel you will be dealing with in the venues you approach. Many theatre managers or venue programmers are diligent, enthusiastic and utterly professional. Too many are none of those things, and a surprising number have no discernible interest in theatre at all.

Firstly, you need to identify the theatres where your work might find an audience. There are thousands of public performing spaces in this country from old community halls to vast modern auditoria, and you should aim at the ones that accommodate small- to medium-scale work. All but the tiniest theatres have a website where you can see their current programme, and often an archive too, where you can check the type of work they present.

Introduce yourself

Your first task is to make them aware of your work. Identify the person who will make the decision to take your show or not and address all your correspondence to him or her. Try and get all the relevant information on a page of A4 or equivalent, and include a description of the show, images, contact details, reviews if you have them, and brief biographies of your creative team. Mail this, or send online, with a personalised letter to the venue manager.

A week or so later you should make a follow-up phone call. You will often be sidetracked to another member of staff or diverted to voicemail. This is where dogged does it. Don't just leave a voicemail and expect a prompt answer. Call back until you are able to have a conversation with the person responsible for booking shows.

Remember that programming probably accounts for less than ten per cent of this individual's workload and that at this stage they won't have time for a long conversation about the artistic merits of what you have to offer. Identify yourself, tell them why you are calling and ask, as a courtesy, if this is an appropriate time to discuss programming. You can be politely persistent, but once it becomes clear that your pitch is not going to work, don't become a nuisance caller. Accept that your work will be more appreciated elsewhere and move on.

You are pushing only one product. The programmer is probably juggling dozens of potential shows and a very complicated budget. You, of course, will want to talk about the quality of the work and convince them that your show will do good business. Have all the relevant details to hand before the conversation and be well prepared to answer any of the questions the promoter may ask you. What the programmer is thinking about, even as he or she warms to the idea of your show, is how much you will want to charge. You will have a preferred figure in mind that will cover your costs and reasonably reward your hard work. You should also have a carefully calculated figure below which it would be impractical to agree. Your fee might be all-inclusive or you may want to negotiate travel and accommodation expenses separately. Be flexible but realistic; you may love your work, but you shouldn't be giving it away at this stage.

If the phone call ends with an expression of interest, but with reservations about the money, you should follow up with as many calls as it takes to negotiate a definite booking and an agreed guaranteed payment. There is sometimes the option of a minimum fee plus an agreed percentage of the box office. This alternative will test your nerve and require even more skilful financial juggling.

As soon as you hang up on that last conversation put something in writing immediately. An appreciative letter or e-mail with the date and time of the performance, the figures agreed for your fee and expenses, and a request for a contract from the venue will at least reiterate that you have reached a settlement.

More definitively you can send a booking confirmation form with more detailed information. This should include:

Your details:

- The name of your company (if you have one).
- Your name.
- The name of the show.
- Contacts: home or business address, landline and mobile phone numbers and e-mail address. A fax number too if available.
- Names and contacts for any personnel you engage, such as your technician or marketing contact.
- Website if applicable.

Venue details:

- The name of the venue.
- The address of the venue.
- Contacts: administration phone, e-mail and website.
- The capacity of the venue.
- Names, contacts numbers and e-mail addresses of relevant venue personnel; management (usually the person you've made the booking through), marketing, technical, education. (The education department is only relevant if you are offering workshops or outreach work alongside your production.)

Performance details:

- Date or dates.
- Performance start time.
- Duration (total performing length with or without interval).
- Performance with or without interval.

- Add-on activities: outreach, education, pre- or post-show discussions.

Financial details:

- The deal – guaranteed fee or split box-office arrangement.
- Terms of payment – bank transfer, cheque, cash.
- Print requirement – how much promotional material, e.g. posters and leaflets, you need to provide, and the date by which the venue should receive them for over-printing and distribution.
- Merchandising: CDs, DVDs, scripts, T-shirts, etc., and the percentage of sales taken by management.

A contract

The theatre's response to this booking confirmation should be their standard contract. Depending on the level of bureaucracy practised at the venue, this can range from a simple two-page document to thirty pages of close print. Much of the longer version will not be relevant to you, but brace yourself and check through all of it for clauses that you hadn't bargained for. You may come across one word there that, if you have not encountered it before, should be added immediately to your vocabulary: contra. Ignore it and it could jump up and bite you on the leg. The contra is what the venue might try to charge you for certain services that you assumed to be covered in the verbal agreement. This might be for the overprinting on the leaflets and posters you supply to the marketing department with the venue's logo and the timing of the performance. Although this is usually covered by the management, don't take it for granted. Likewise, be sure you will not be charged for extra technical staff to set-up, run and do the get-out for your show.

Keep in contact

There may be a long gap between the two signatures on the contract and your performance. In a busy or badly run organisation you might not have the priority you deserve, so it is up to you to maintain contact and reassure yourself that all is going to plan. With your contract, or before, you should have received details of the theatre's technical specifications, which will relate to matters such as stage dimensions, what lighting and sound equipment is available, and how many staff will be at your disposal. In turn you should send the technical contact clear and easily accessible details of your requirements in plenty of time. If you are not touring with a technician who can do this for you, and you are not competent to do it yourself, be sure to enlist the help of somebody who is, because you should be blameless in the event of any shortcomings on the day. Check long before arriving that your technical contact at the theatre doesn't anticipate any problems.

Be vigilant

A call to the marketing department a month or so before your performance will not only confirm that they have received your publicity materials but might also remind them to put extra effort into promoting your show. You are entitled to ask how seats are selling and you should offer yourself up for local newspaper or radio interviews to stimulate interest. Even if your fee is guaranteed, you don't want to play to a poor house, and evidence of strong ticket sales can really help when negotiating future bookings.

At some point check on the theatre website that their information matches yours. It's not uncommon for the wrong starting time to be posted there, and frequently there are spelling mistakes in the play's title, or the names of one of the creative team. It's not good for the ego to discover that someone with a name bearing a resemblance to your own is starring in your play instead of you.

These are mistakes you can rectify with a little vigilance, but when you arrive at the theatre it's too late to point out that your posters or leaflets are nowhere in evidence and there seems to be no indication that you are playing there that very night. There is really no excuse for these errors or sins of omission but they happen often enough to make me wary of the standard of publicity and marketing departments in theatres of all sizes in this country. I suppose if the personnel were any good at high-octane selling they'd be doing it somewhere other than at an arts venue and on a much better salary. You also need to face the ugly reality that your show might be a quota-filler at a venue that usually presents tribute bands, pantos and the local amateurs, but is required to have some 'art' in their programme from time to time. You are the 'art', you're relatively cheap and only there for one night so not worth expending too much energy on. When you come across a well-run, efficient and welcoming theatre this cynicism melts with the warmth of their welcome and whatever size house you play to, you know you are valued.

This sequence of approaching, contracting and maintaining contact will apply to all the dates you aim to fill.

Publicity

Design

The quality of your printed publicity is crucial, as is choosing the right graphic designer to work with. Economise on something else if you have to, but always engage a graphic artist with experience of print publicity for the theatre. He or she will need to understand the ramifications of enlarging or diminishing the chosen image and how important it is to make the printed information on the design legible as well as attractive.

You should budget between £400 and £1,000 for the flyer and poster design, and get quotes from at least five designers whose work you like. Recommendation is the surest way to find the right designer, and you can also study current publicity material and find which style appeals to you and is appropriate for your work. If you see a design you like, contact the company producing that show and ask for the designer's name and contact details.

The image

What would be the most effective and memorable image for your show – a photograph in character, a representative or abstract illustration, a cartoon or simply the name of the show boldly executed? Discuss options with your designer and ask for rough versions of what appeals to you. He or she will almost certainly have ideas of their own, so be open to their experienced opinions whilst holding out for your own vision.

Even when you're presented with imaginative responses to your brief you must be exacting and accept finished artwork only when it is right in every detail. As the responsibility for the finished product will be yours, you should always be the final arbiter on how your show is promoted.

The copy

Once the image has captured their attention, your potential audience will want a brief and compelling description of the show, so take painstaking care over the copy you give your designer.

As when choosing your image, do extensive research by checking out copy on leaflets and brochures for other shows. Do they give an immediate impression of what the show is about? Will the audience be in for a light-hearted evening, or something more profound? Is the show aimed at a particular type of audience or age group? Apply these criteria to your own show, so that your copy will answer those questions quickly and clearly.

Your first attempt to do full justice to your work may run into several hundred words, but remember the dimensions of the leaflet, the size of the print, and the amount of time a potential punter will be prepared to give your publicity material. Rewrite the copy aiming to make it half the length, but with twice the impact, and then repeat the process until you have a lean, punchy few lines that make your show appear unmissable.

Hyberbole has its place, but use it sparingly and without losing credibility. An experienced theatregoer will sniff out exaggerated claims and avoid you. Some publicists, sensitive to the antipathy of many towards solo plays, will devise copy that almost disguises the genre. If not dishonest, this is certainly not helpful in the long run. The words 'solo', 'one-man' or 'one-woman' should certainly feature and be celebrated.

Market research

At its various stages of development, ask the opinions of people you respect on the impact of your image and copy. Others in your creative team will obviously have ideas but they will not be impartial, so spread your net to include other professionals, as well as those who go to see plays but may not have in-depth experience of the process.

Ultimately the show will stand or fall by the quality of your performance, but before that verdict is passed, your print can have as much influence on your potential audience as the title of your play, with a similar power to alienate or attract.

Flyers and posters will be what venues require, but you can use the same image and edited copy on postcards, leaflets and your website, if you have one.

Flyers

These will customarily be on A5-size paper. You should aim at one strong image on the front with the title of your piece in large letters. Your name and that of your writer, if you have one, should be prominent and any other members of your creative team, if you feel they are 'sellable'. If not, credit them on the reverse. If you have a good press quote this should also feature on the front.

Leave a blank strip on the bottom of the flyer for over-printing details of the venue, dates and times of the performances, and a box-office telephone number or website.

The back of the flyer should have a clear and interesting explanation of what the show is about, more press quotes if you have them, and creative-team credits and sponsors' logos, if required.

Posters

The same image should appear on your posters, which will typically be A3 paper size. Like the flyer you should include press quotes, sponsorship logos and whichever artistic credits you can, without overcrowding the space. A blank strip for overprinting is also required on the poster.

Quantities

The amount of print you need will be stipulated by what the venues require. As a standard estimate, a touring venue will require 1,000 flyers and 40–50 posters. Some will request fewer and some will ask for up to 2,500 flyers and 100 posters. Before complying with this larger amount do question the number with the venue, as it's not uncommon to arrive and find some of your print in an unopened box in the marketing department's office. It's a waste of paper and your budget.

When ordering your print you will find it much more economical to pay for a long print run, and be sure to get estimates from a number of printers to get the best deal. Don't, however, compromise on the quality of the paper used; a light and flimsy leaflet will look cheap in a rack of similar but higher specification material. A 'droopy' flyer will not inspire confidence.

Websites

You can take advantage of the increasing popularity of websites as a marketing tool for your show. Most graphic designers are now capable of creating websites too, so you might be able to use the same designer for your print and your web presence. Alternatively, look at other sites and approach the designers of those you like for estimates.

The first cost is buying the domain name you want to represent your show. This has actually become less expensive than previously, and you can buy a .co.uk domain for around £10, with a .com domain costing twice that. After that, decide whether you want a basic site or something more sophisticated and compare costs.

As important as creating the site is updating it. For your show this might mean including new booking dates, your latest reviews, even a blog. An outdated site will reflect badly on your work, so either get your designer to upgrade it regularly, or to save money do it yourself using a content management system (CMS) such as WordPress.

Though a useful addition to your publicity armoury, a website is not a substitute for good quality print in a well-presented information pack.

Photographs

Photographs of you to publicise the show will be required either for your print publicity and/or media packs. Just as you only need one good photo from a shoot for your entry in *Spotlight*, so a single image can sell your show. Getting the right image is worth the investment of a professional photographer.

Don't expect the photographer to come along and dictate the session. It's up to you or the director to choose the locations, the type of photographs and what you want them to express. Even so, you should try and schedule time for some more spontaneous shots that were not part of your original plan in case that delivers a maverick image that you end up loving and using.

Depending on the photographer you choose and how much of their time you need, a photoshoot can cost you between £250 and £1,500. If this is impossible to reconcile with your budget, then a gifted amateur might come up with the goods but be sure they provide you with images of at least 300dpi (generally 1MB in size).

Booking Agencies

You may be daunted by the prospect of so much administrative work on top of the artistic energy demanded of you by your show, and prefer to hand it over to an experienced booking management. There aren't so many of them that you will be spoilt for choice, and not all agencies handle solo work. Browse the web for one-person shows you have seen or heard of and find out who represents them. If you know someone with a show already on the road, check out their experience of their booker and ask if they would recommend your approaching them. There is quite a high percentage of players who move from agency to agency in the hope of improving their hit rate, and, as with many actors' agencies, some performers feel their work is not marketed aggressively enough.

It would be unusual for a booker to take on a piece of work that they hadn't seen, so use some forethought and invite them to a performance as soon as you feel confident of your work. If they believe in your show, discuss with them what sort of future they envisage for it, and think about whether it comes close to your own expectations.

Some managements work on a prepaid-fee basis, and others on a commission, so think through the financial implications. The payments they ask may seem disproportionate, but if they can get you work you couldn't access yourself then you'll be better off taking their deal than hanging on to your one hundred per cent of nothing.

There will be a contract between you and your booker, which you should read with scrupulous care and which should also be read by a third party with your best interests at heart. As ever, the devil will be in the detail and missing out on even the most insignificant-looking detail could lead to problems and resentments as the relationship with your booking agent continues.

PROFILE

Mark Makin, makin projects

Mark heads his own company, partnered by his wife Penny and an administrative assistant, based in Cheltenham. From early touring experience as a roadie and merchandiser for music groups and comics, he joined one of the larger producing agencies, UK Arts International, as a tour booker. Almost six years on he had gained invaluable experience working on domestic and worldwide tours for high-profile companies and individuals, including the solo work of Steven Berkoff and Linda Marlowe.

After a period on the sharp end as general manager of a dance company, Mark returned to tour management as his own boss, and now handles an eclectic stable of artists including hip-hop and contemporary-dance theatre, small- to large-scale theatre companies, and several solo performers.

His championing of one-person shows is based on a genuine enthusiasm for the genre and a belief that, at its best, it is the purest form of theatre. Mark puts his money where his mouth is and now co-produces as well as promotes some of the solo work he represents.

Acknowledging that a solo play with a well-known or recognisable theme or a proven performer is likelier to have a longer shelf-life, he also champions the new and less resilient pieces of work that have a shorter life but no less powerful impact.

For work that Mark admires but doesn't feel he has time or resources to fully manage, he will occasionally act as mentor and offer practical help and advice to the actor to assume responsibility for booking their own work. He also offers consultancies to individuals or small groups on the complexities of selling a show successfully. His sessions deal with the basics of company structure, budgeting for touring, promotional packs, supplying sample paperwork and identifying appropriate markets for the work in question.

The Edinburgh Festival Fringe

Playing the Edinburgh Festival Fringe

To put your show on the map, generate press interest, and exploit opportunities for future bookings you don't have to play the Edinburgh Festival Fringe. But doing it can tick all those boxes at once, and though it has been likened to standing under a cold shower tearing up £50 notes, you should do it at least once, if only to boast that you survived the experience.

If you've visited the Festival as a patron or even flicked through the Fringe brochure you'll know the scale of the largest open-access arts festival in the world, and you'll have realised with how many events your show will be in competition. One thing you won't have to worry about, though, is any sort of selection process. If you have a show, can find a venue for it and can pay to put it on, nobody can stop you performing at the Festival, which of course explains why so much of what gets on is rubbish.

Your offering will be one of around two and a half thousand entertainments to choose from in Edinburgh during the month of August. Old hands will have their fears confirmed that the theatre element of the Fringe is slowly but inexorably being subsumed by stand-up comedy which now accounts for nearly forty per cent of the shows on offer, ten per cent more than theatre pieces.

A producer may handle the whole business of taking your show to Edinburgh, if you are lucky enough to have one. If you are doing it yourself then it's reassuring to know that the Fringe Society can help you out on virtually every aspect of the process (www.edfringe.com). They will warn you, too, that the revenue you generate is more than likely not enough to cover your outlay, which is a timely alert as much of that outlay will be going their way.

Planning ahead

Timescale is all-important because Edinburgh is not a mountain you can climb on a whim. At the end of one Festival, plans and preparations are already under way for the next year. You'll be at a huge advantage if you have already visited the Festival at least once as a punter, or part of a larger performing group. This gives you the chance to check out venues, and their locations. City-centre spaces are bound to be more expensive, but also consider the size of auditorium, the shape of stage and the relationship with the audience that best suits your work. Technical facilities will also vary greatly from venue to venue, and take into consideration the expense of importing technical equipment and employing personnel to operate it. If possible, talk to the participants who are using the spaces you favour to learn the pros and cons from their experience.

A few days' visit will also help you come to terms with how expensive the city is during August, remind you to pack plenty of warm, waterproof clothes at the height of a Scottish summer, and test-run your liver.

Once life north of the border is returning to normal after Hogmanay you should be contacting your favoured venues and discovering whether they are within your budget. By February you should have firmed up on where you will be performing and, almost as important, when you will be performing. For a show aimed at children, the morning is often a good bet, and less in demand from Festival diehards for whom dawn is almost synonymous with bedtime. The evening, when local audiences are free after work, is most in demand especially by stand-ups, so between noon and six o' clock is a primetime for drama.

By March you should be submitting your registration form for inclusion in the Fringe, which means having a lot of detailed information about the what, where and when of your show. This is not a job for Luddites, as the form can only be sent online. You will also be asked to submit a description of the show's content for the official programme, and an image to accompany it. If you're not good at précis get some help with this, as it's very taxing to encapsulate all the great things you want to say about your work in the maximum forty words allowed. And if you haven't already gasped at the cost of hiring the venue and securing accommodation, be prepared to go into shock at the price of this minimal but essential publicity, and then risk a coronary when you consider buying an eye-catching advert in the same publication. There'll be plenty more financial shocks to come but don't delay payment beyond the deadline in April. Come June the puff for your show will have been printed and distributed in 400,000 copies of the Fringe Programme.

Print publicity will be your next major outlay and the quantities of leaflets and posters required to be able to compete with other companies will seem staggering and globally irresponsible. Grit your teeth and insist on the printer using recycled paper or card.

Finding your audience

Getting people to see your work is the next priority after ensuring that it's worth seeing. Your best option is to hire an experienced press agent to publicise your show to the media. Every year the Fringe office compiles a list of such agents. You should engage one to get working with you after you have confirmed your venue, but before the Fringe programme is launched.

The agent will write your press release and liaise with newspapers and online writers to maximise your coverage, increase the likelihood of your work being previewed and reviewed, and raise the profile of your show in the media at every opportunity.

Good press agents are expensive, though, and if your budget doesn't stretch that far, be prepared for some serious slog. Detailed advice on how to write your press release, when to submit it and how to follow it up are available on the official Fringe website and from their Media Office; these are your most valuable resources on how to do things effectively and when. They can offer guidance on every aspect of your media and marketing campaign, including what images to use and which media organisations you need to target. They will advise you on how to invite critics to your show and how to persevere if they seem reluctant to review you. You can even approach them for support if things are getting too much for you.

What you do between now and your opening performance, apart from getting the show into tip-top shape, depends on your ingenuity and perseverance. Start a blog, network on Facebook or Twitter, and pull any strings you can in the media.

Accommodation

Somewhere to lay your head in central Edinburgh is outrageously priced during the Festival, and you should have booked your accommodation as early as possible because, unlike package holidays, there are rarely any last-minute bargains. Some people advocate staying on the outskirts or even commuting from the relatively low-priced cultural centre of Glasgow to save money. I think this misses half the point of the Festival, which is to be truly a part of it and totally immersed in the experience. There are several websites (e.g. www.festivalflats.net) that list accommodation available during the Festival.

Strutting your stuff

Performing your show once a day, seven days a week for a month, with possibly only one or two days off during that period, will be the main focus for your energy. Your venue will be cramming in as many shows as possible to make money, and the time for your get-in and get-out will be very limited. If your play spills over its allotted time-slot many venues will charge a penalty, so you'll need to exercise military precision.

Backstage

Dressing-room space will be limited and oversubscribed so be as self-contained in your allotted corner as possible, and be very aware of security. You'll be out of that room for the duration of the play with no fellow artist to keep an eye on your possessions. Valuables and money go missing with depressing frequency in a busy and not properly secured building and your insurance won't cover any losses if you have been negligent. That prop or period hat that you imagined would be of no interest to anyone else can also disappear and sabotage your show, so find locked cupboards or suitcases for everything between performances.

You may also find that there is no access to a lavatory once you are behind your real or metaphorical footlights, so don't get caught short.

After the show

When the show is over for the day you'll have time to schmooze, network and watch other companies' work. You'll have no excuse for not knowing what else is going on and where to find it with the ubiquitous print literature, and there is even an app for the iPhone (produced by the Fringe Office) that will all but take you there by the hand.

Every season there are new areas around major performing sites that theme themselves for eating, drinking and mixing with fellow performers and your potential public. As a one-man band this social jungle can be rather intimidating, but you have to think of it as part of the job and promote the show in any way you can. If you're uninhibited and adventurous there are parades and stunts you can join in, endless opportunities for leafleting and talking about the show to potential punters on the Royal Mile or whilst queuing up to see other shows. Radio interviews and features in the specialist Festival press can all enhance your profile, though you will be in competition with the thousands of others seeking the same coverage.

Critics

Word of mouth will certainly help improve your chances of good houses, but there is one indisputable fact that defines the difference between success and failure at the Festival, and that is the critical attention your show gets. There are still some adventurous souls willing to take a punt on a show that simply tickles their fancy, but most festivalgoers will be relying on the newspapers, free sheets and websites to advise them on what not to miss and what to avoid. The invidious star system means that some won't even be bothered to read a review, but simply accept its stellar rating.

A five-star review in *The Scotsman* – or winning a coveted Fringe First from the same publication – will catapult your show into the top-seller league. Make sure you shout it from the rooftops, put banners on your publicity material, add it to your website and let every other media outlet know about it. Getting the accolade is a wonderful endorsement, but *when* you get it is crucial. Shows are reviewed throughout the Festival so a star-studded review during the first week can make the difference between profit or loss, but if you're only acknowledged at the tail-end of the month your ego may be boosted, but you'll still have the legacy of patchy houses to cope with. This is a fact of the Edinburgh experience and there is nothing you can do about it. Just hope that other critics will get to you earlier, appreciate your work and boost your box-office.

One of the problems with theatre criticism at the Festival is that there are so many shows to cover there aren't enough competent, experienced critics in the country to give each the attention it deserves. The reputable ones are probably giving priority to the high-profile shows and the rest are rooky, aspiring young critics who are sometimes more interested in self-promotion than fulfilling their function. Having said that, you will be desperate to get even one of these wannabes to give your show a good review.

Encountering this coverage, or lack of it, may be the first time you've had such a close-up and personal connection with people who hold the future of your show in their hands. One incontrovertible truth about any critic who attends your solo show is that they won't be able to ignore you.

Tyne Daly (Detective Lacey in the US TV series *Cagney and Lacey* for those old enough to remember) said, 'A critic is someone who never actually goes to the battle, yet who afterwards comes out shooting the wounded.' Most artists, including almost everyone connected with the performing arts, despise critics. In the theatre it's not unknown to encounter people we dislike or find difficult; a bullying director, a selfish actor, a megalomaniac designer can all make our lives harder. Our solution may be to confront them or, if that's not possible, to share our experiences of them within the theatre community in the hope that we can revenge ourselves on their reputations. With a critic this redress is not possible because they are unreachable, impervious and always have the last word. Alas, the critic who sinks your show from ignorance, lack of perception, or the desire to show off will stay with you for ever, just as those five stars will. It's easier said than done, but try and keep it in proportion.

Edinburgh may be your only opportunity ever to get a critic from the national press to come and see your show. On a UK tour your audience might be impressed by Scottish acclaim but seeing a quote from a newspaper they read themselves will have a lot more impact. Accolades from *The Guardian, The Telegraph, The Independent* or any of the Sundays can legitimately proclaim your success for the life of the show. After Edinburgh your future is likely to be one- or two-night stands in regional venues where even the local press might not attend. Playing a two- or three-week run in a London fringe venue may not persuade the nationals to cover you either, as they will regard your shelf-life as too short to warrant an evening of their time.

What's in it for you?

All your efforts and the coruscating quality of your work might pay off, get you full houses, five-star reviews, a Fringe First and the Best Solo Performer Award from *The Stage*. If it does one of the above you'll have every reason to celebrate. The alternative of dismal audiences, no press coverage and total indifference from award panels doesn't necessarily mean you've wasted your time. If you're serious about an afterlife for your show, the presence of enthusiastic venue managers, booking agents or an overseas scout or two is just as important.

And although Edinburgh is the biggest and most important arts festival in the UK, there are dozens of other
festivals that you can approach to take your work. For the
best overview and an excellent search engine look at
www.artsfestivals.co.uk. There is also a list of festivals likely
to take solo work in the Appendix.

Life After Edinburgh

Take stock and move on

Whether you leave Edinburgh exhilarated or downcast, you will almost certainly leave out of pocket and exhausted. But now is not the time to pause for breath. Immediately follow up on any interest that managements or individuals might have taken in your show. If they don't already have your information pack, despatch it immediately and update your website if you have one. Add the good notices you may have got, and if you don't have any then quote positive audience feedback. One artful friend of mine got no press coverage whatever, but a visitor from Aberdeen who saw his play told him it was the best show on the Fringe. His publicity appeared with a banner: ' "This is the best show on the Fringe" *Scotsman*.' Well, the punter *was* a Scotsman.

Lick your wounds and bemoan your overdraft in front of friends, but to the profession you must put a positive gloss on your Edinburgh experience.

Juggling dates

Try and get confirmations from venues as outlined earlier, and be as flexible as you can about dates. Don't expect your putative tour to make any geographical sense. Having accepted a gig in Bangor on January 10th, you might find yourself offered another in Bognor on January 12th. Accept the booking and worry about the logistics later. If you have a tour booker they should be experienced enough to try and negotiate a more sensible itinerary without jeopardising the booking, but that is juggling for professional jugglers.

Keep it fresh

The gap between Edinburgh and the next paid engagement for your show may be a matter of months and you will have to handle the interregnum stoically. Apart from keeping body and soul together, you must also keep the show fresh so it will be ready to bounce back to vibrant life when required. Run the lines regularly, preferably with a patient friend on the book, to sharpen your concentration. Use the time to learn from the mistakes you may have become aware of during the Edinburgh run, simplify elements of the production which could be usefully refined, economising your use of furniture, props and costumes without losing the production values you aim for.

Preparing to tour

A very practical use of your time would be to finalise the technical script you will be taking out on tour. If you are travelling with a technician, interpreting this script will be their responsibility. They are professional so aim to make your script likewise, and if necessary enlist the help of an experienced touring technician to compile it. If you are travelling alone, a clear, uncluttered and easily interpreted script will speed up your technical rehearsals on tour, and endear you to the venue's staff.

As you are a solo item you should design your technical requirements so that one technician, responsible for both lighting and sound, can operate the show. Some venues will provide two as a matter of course, but others will either not have the staff available or will want to charge you extra for a second operator. Remember the contra.

A master script

The first pages of the script should have drawn or computer-generated diagrams of the playing area you utilise, along with length, breadth and depth measurements, preferably in metres. These should show the relative positions of any furniture or static props that you use, and the coverage of whatever general lighting states you need, together with an indication of the gel colours required. For particular lighting effects indicate where the 'specials' should be located and their spread on the playing area.

Aim the script at the least competent operator you might encounter, not the genius you hope for. Colour-coding light and sound cues with highlighter is a useful ploy, and very helpful if cues are simultaneous. With only one actor, your script will probably look more like a piece of prose than a conventional play, so embolden and put in capitals your stage directions and any visual cues you use to differentiate them from your spoken text.

You will mostly be playing one-night stands so this script of yours is going to pass through many hands over the length of a successful tour. Each venue you play will have slightly different equipment, and this can affect the timing of some or all of your cues. Every technician writing the differentiations onto your pages will mean your pristine script will end up looking more like a scruffy palimpsest. You will only have yourself to blame if a busy technician who has had your script in his hands for just a few hours makes a mistake by acting on one of your previous technician's interpolations.

The answer is to laminate the pages once your script is finalised, put it in a strong folder, and supply your operators with Post-it notes to alter the cues to suit themselves.

It's easy to forget things in the post-show bustle as you rush to finish the get-out at the theatre and get in to the bar, but of all the things not to leave behind, the show's master script is the most crucial. Just in case, be sure to have a spare one at home and a copy saved on your computer.

Touring

Getting there

The only thing you can be certain of on a tour of one-night stands is that every one will be different. Variety is great and will keep you on your toes, but it also takes its toll on your resources so forward-planning and preparedness are vital.

Unless your show fits into a suitcase and you intend to rely on public transport you will be travelling in a vehicle driven by you or your technician. Make sure the vehicle is in good condition, and check for screen wash and sufficient petrol before leaving base.

Allow plenty of time for the unexpected problem or unscheduled delay, and if your transport doesn't have an in-built satellite-navigation system, buying one would be a good investment. Major theatres are easy to locate, but schools, community halls and small arts centres can be very elusive, and frantically driving round in circles is not how an actor prepares. If the venue is far enough away from your base to warrant travelling the day before your performance give yourself the peace of mind of staying in a hotel or guest house, especially if you have negotiated some expenses into your contract.

Have you got everything?

Have a checklist of everything you will need for the show. As it's easy to lose lists, keep yours on laminated card, and make sure there are copies. Double check that everything is packed; smaller items, like the CD or digital file of your incidental music or the gobos you require, are more easily overlooked. Don't compromise your work by having to make do without them.

Don't leave home either without the contact numbers of the venue personnel you will be dealing with, in case of any problem or emergency. Add them to the contacts on your mobile phone.

You will have arranged a time to start your get-in and be sure to check beforehand about parking arrangements at or near the venue so that you will be punctual and not come back to a parking ticket slapped on your windscreen. If you're travelling with a technician he or she might be glad to have you out of the way once you've helped with the get-in so they can get on with their work, but if it's just you and a strange crew or individual operator then there are certain guidelines you can observe to get the best out of them.

Polish your people skills

It's polite to memorise the names of the technical staff before your arrival and, as you are a visitor on their turf, to establish as civil a working relationship as possible. As with actors you will find a huge disparity in the capabilities of technicians, but alienating them when you discover their incompetence will not help if you are relying on them to run your show proficiently. They do, after all, have their finger on the button.

If no one from the theatre management or front-of-house team makes themselves known to you (it does happen), go and make your presence known to them, and let them know how pleased you are to be playing their venue.

Getting to love the tech

Hanging the lights is the most time-consuming preparation for your show. Conscientious staff will have received your lighting plan and done this before your arrival, but the speed of the turnaround in a very busy venue sometimes defeats even the most efficient crew; so don't take this for granted. In ideal circumstances they will also have done a rough focus of your general states and specials so that you will need only to finesse these and get on with plotting the show.

It's possible you may never have had reason to go into a lighting and sound control booth before, but you should look at the stage from the same point of view as your operator. Check lighting states from here and from the auditorium as well as from the stage, and be clear and definite about your decisions. You don't want to confirm what most technicians think of actors.

When setting your sound levels, listen from several vantage points in the auditorium, especially from close to the speakers if they are positioned front of house. Find a balance where cues are effective from the back seats but not deafening from the front.

If you travel with a laptop, you can harness developing technology to make your sound operation even easier. There are software programmes for both Mac (QLab) and PC (SFX) where you can record your sound cues for direct transmission through the venue's sound system.

As well as offering your sound operative an easy cueing system for your music and effects, you save time by having the sound levels preprogrammed. This obviates the need for a session to set levels afresh at every venue and makes cueing errors infinitely less likely.

A tip

In some theatres it is possible to get a really effective black-out, which is good news but has an attendant hazard. If you are 'discovered' on stage, or walk off in darkness there is always the chance of you missing your mark or tripping over a stage weight. Take some luminous tape with you to give you the security of knowing where to aim for and when to stop. Richer theatres might provide you with a little (it is unbelievably expensive) but not all stock it or have some to spare so take your own. And remember to reclaim it after the show; it's reusable.

Cue-to-cue

Once you are satisfied with lighting and sound levels you can decide to do a full dress rehearsal if there is time, or cut cue-to-cue if time is limited or you want to conserve your energy. There will be a statutory break for technical staff between your rehearsal and the half-hour before the show so use your time efficiently.

Before the show

What you do with the remaining period before the show will depend on your personal routine and rhythms. Some actors are actually able to eat, others will want fresh air or a rest back at the hotel or in the dressing room. Whichever suits you, first try and get the stage and auditorium to yourself for half an hour or so. In the Greek theatre this would have been known as making the space sacred, and it is your opportunity to acquaint yourself with every inch of the playing area, test your voice at its most powerful and at its most hushed, and range your eyes over every seat in the house. Go into the auditorium and view the stage from every row, not just the central seats but the extremities and the restricted views, the back of the house and the upper reaches in a large space. Check those sightlines rigorously; if the audience can't see you then there is nothing else for them to look at and it's an old but true adage that if they can't see you, they can't hear you either.

After the show

A cooperative crew or individual technician will offer to help you with the get-out. You'll be tired and grateful but remember to use your checklist scrupulously, and take ultimate responsibility for packing up your props and costumes. Don't leave without those items that will have spent the show in the control room – your sound CD, lighting gobos, and of course the all-important master script.

Theatre manners matter

If things have gone well, find the time to write a letter of appreciation to the venue and name particular members of staff who were helpful. You may want to go back. If things have gone wrong, write as diplomatic a letter as you can. You may want to go back.

Budgeting

Here is a sample budget for a one-night-stand performance, giving a realistic fee and costs.

Income	
Venue fee	£800
TOTAL	£800
Touring expenditure	
Performer fee	£150
Technical manager fee	£150
Travel day fees (if applicable)	£50
Per diem – technical manager	£15
Per diem – performer	£15
Poster and flyer postage to venue	£30
Accommodation – performer (£45 per person per night)	£45
Accommodation – technical manager	£45
Travel (trains/taxis/bus/etc.)	£60
Parking	£10
Misc. consumable props	£15
Tech consumables (gels/hook clamps/LX/etc.)	£40
Car/van hire	£50
Fuel	£75
Insurance	£50
PRS	N/A
TOTAL	£800
CURRENT INCOME	£800
CURRENT EXPENDITURE	£800
PROFIT/DEFICIT	£0

Bear in mind that the average fees for your show that you can expect from venues are anything between a box-office split to average guaranteed fees between £350 and £900.

To make some performances work on the fees available from venues you may decide that you'll compromise on your own fee to make a small venue fee work for you.

Savings can be made if:

- You do not need to hire a car or van so you can travel on a pre-booked train.

- No car/van equals no fuel costs either.

- You don't need a technical manager to operate your show.

- Accommodation – if you return to home base after a performance (if the travel distance is not too great) or if you stay with friends/family whilst on tour.

- You may decide that a per diem (daily allowance) is not required.

- Note that tax and National Insurance does not get taken from per diems.

Value Added Tax

If you are already paying Value Added Tax (VAT) you will be familiar with the advantages and disadvantages of being registered. There is a threshold of turnover that would make you liable to pay VAT, and at the time of writing that was £73,000 per annum. You can register voluntarily if your income is below this, but you need to balance the benefits of this with the amount of extra book-keeping work for you or your accountant. You'll find advice and guidance on the relevant website: www.hmrc.gov.uk.

Remember, if you are registered, to quote this at the time of negotiating a booking. For venues that are not VAT registered, or exempt from paying tax, this can be a problem as they will have to find that extra 20% (at current rates) on top of your fee. There may be occasions where this proves too expensive and you may have to compromise on your fee or lose the engagement.

Rural Touring

Small can be beautiful

One very extensive and promising touring circuit is the network of rural venues that operate throughout England and Wales. Village halls and community centres host nearly four thousand performances by professional companies every year and operate via forty regional Rural Touring schemes. They are represented by the National Rural Touring Forum and full details are available on their website: www.nrtf.org.uk. As well as the extensive information you will find there, you can also register details of your show online, and download their practical guides to rural touring.

Your vital contact within the organisation is the promoter who will select your show, market it and host the evening. These promoters are unpaid volunteers not professional arts staff so your dealings will be even less predictable than with conventional venues. The performing spaces they deal with range from the primitive to the sophisticated, so flexibility and adaptability will be your watchwords.

Starting with your nearest touring scheme you should contact them to ask for any information about their programme and in return give details of your work and why you think it would be suitable for rural touring. Alert them to any planned performances that they might be able to attend to assess your show.

The information pack you send will need to have additional information to the one that you supply to theatres and arts centres. Taking into account the technical limitations of many potential performing spaces, you should specify your absolute minimum performing space, including height for those halls with low ceilings or roof beams. If you are taking your own lighting and sound equipment, for example, it's essential to know how many 13-amp plugs the venue offers and what the sightlines are like if you find yourself playing on a flat floor.

What did they think of the show?

Rural communities may not be representative of your usual audience and you will need to be sensitive to their expectations of a show in their local hall. After the performance they may be eager to tell you how much they enjoyed it, but they'll also feel entitled to express the opposite opinion, so diplomacy and broad shoulders are required. If you need accommodation that could well be in a local B&B, but you might find yourself hosted in the promoter's own home, and that could add an unscheduled social event to your itinerary.

If, after your first foray onto the rural-touring circuit, you want to pursue it, you should be sure to ask for evaluations of your work and as much feedback from audience and promoters as you can get.

Criminal record checks are important if your work involves contact with children or vulnerable adults, and you can find out more from www.crb.gov.uk.

International Touring

Seeing the world

You will acquire a remarkable degree of resilience and adaptability as you take your show around the UK. These are qualities you will need in abundance if you contemplate touring abroad. When things don't go smoothly at home there is always a support network of friends or colleagues you can turn to, and you are rarely more than half a day away from base. Apart from impenetrable dialects you will have no language problems, the weather holds few surprises, and neither do the food or the customs of the locals. If you tour internationally, the safety net of the familiar is whisked away and you will have a whole raft of new challenges to cope with, as well as having to maintain the calibre of your work.

You are likely also to be exposed to some life-changing experiences, meet remarkable people, enrich your craft and be humbled by the richness of different cultures. If you get the chance to tour overseas, you should grab it with both hands.

Apart from your desire to travel, you will need a show that travels well too. If globetrotting was always part of your master plan you may have tried to second guess this and tailored your play for just such opportunities. If you want to find out what shows are finding favour in other countries you should become acquainted with the British Council and its Drama and Dance departments.

The British Council

It's possible you have never heard of the British Council. It describes itself as Britain's international cultural-relations body 'connecting the UK to the world and the world to the UK'. Visit the website (www.britishcouncil.org) and navigate around its Arts section. Its annual publication, *Performance in Profile*, also available online, lists companies whose work it feels able to endorse as suitable for overseas touring, along with their current projects, touring availability, target audience, personnel and technical requirements.

The Drama and Dance departments have specific targets of their own. The audience they aim at primarily is described as 'young adults', defined as between the ages of sixteen and thirty-five. Working in almost every part of the world the Council are especially keen to promote the performing arts in the Islamic world, China, sub-Saharan Africa and the newer member states of the European Union.

Understandably they work well in advance, typically a year or more, and have a team of London-based officers with different global responsibilities. These officers assess the work on offer and liaise with the countries they deal with to match product with place and the budgets available. They would never consider sending work abroad under their auspices that had not been seen and approved, but they obviously recognise the economic and logistical advantages of a solo show.

From Edinburgh to the world

The British Council's biennial Edinburgh Showcase is the surest way to get your show in the marketplace. Over two hundred international programmers, venue and festival directors representing over fifty countries experience what Sally Cowling, former Director of Drama and Dance, called 'the fantastic madness' of the Festival. Like registering for the Fringe itself, you will need to plan well ahead, starting with an invitation to attend your show, preferably at least nine months ahead of the event. The response to your invitation may be a refusal because of the suitability of what you are offering, but even if the comeback is more encouraging don't rely on the attendance of anyone as a matter of course. Offer as many options as you can to view your work, so you are leaving as few excuses as possible to miss it. Send reminders and updates on your work that will prompt them to respond. Draw attention to the elements in your show that appeal to their priorities as listed, and be sure to stress any educational or outreach element you can offer in addition to performance.

If your show is accepted for the Showcase it will be offered, along with all the other entries, as an option to the overseas representatives, and the British Council will book and pay for their seats. As well as them turning up for your show there are usually functions and working breakfasts organised for participants, where you can meet and network with the British Council staff and their visitors. This is a chance to flex your ambassadorial muscles as well as promote your work.

It can be months, sometimes years, before representatives abroad invite you to their country, so it is important to update the British Council if you have altered, suspended or abandoned your solo work.

The obvious advantage of touring under the auspices of the British Council is that they offer you the security of working for a government-funded body with vast experience in the regions where they operate. Their contracts are straightforward and unequivocal, but reassure yourself that the scheduling is not overtaxing and that travel arrangements leave you sufficient time to acclimatise. These issues are best resolved before you leave, as once overseas you will need to be as flexible as possible under unfamiliar working conditions. Especially in far-flung places there will be glitches, frustrations, as well as situations and people that try your patience. Those ambassadorial muscles will come in very handy in such situations.

The same advice as in domestic touring applies on the submission of technical specifications, though you may sometimes have to compromise on your production values. Be prepared also to submit your script well in advance to the censor in certain jurisdictions, even if you cannot imagine what might cause offence in your play.

If you have particular dietary requirements be sure to make them known in advance, and the best-organised hosts will often issue a questionnaire about any particular requests at the accommodation or venue. On a ten-city tour of India I had been asked what I would like provided in the dressing room. The last British Council artist, Steven Berkoff, had asked for a particular brand of champagne and towels of a certain size. They were quite curious to meet me as I'd asked for four litres of water and a bunch of bananas. 'We half-expected a thirsty monkey to turn up' was how they greeted me.

Helping your audience

Your performances may be to audiences for whom English is, at best, their second language, so be prepared for some adjustment in the pace of your playing, and be very vigilant about vocal clarity.

If sub- or surtitles are being employed, insist on sufficient rehearsals with the surtitle operatives so that they know where your pauses are and don't end up ruining your laughs by displaying the punchline before you've delivered it. Simultaneous translations are sometimes offered, and you should talk through the script with the translator, as well as requiring at least one full runthrough to familiarise them with your performance. These processes can be helped hugely if your hosts have received a full DVD recording of your performance in good time. This need not be an expensive broadcast-quality item, but could be a single-camera record of the play, preferably in performance.

In some cultures, audience behaviour is very different from ours at its best, and talking through your show or getting up and arbitrarily leaving the auditorium are not uncommon. It's more than likely that what they are talking about is you, and that the wandering audience member will make a noisy re-entrance and ask their neighbour what they have missed, so try not to take it personally.

Remember that you have been invited overseas to work, and showing you a good time is not a compulsory part of your hosts' brief. In my experience you can take generous hospitality, an eagerness to share their culture and a helpful response to any problems as the norm, but there are exceptions. Having travelled possibly halfway across the world you may want to make the most of it, so you should negotiate beforehand about taking unpaid days for sightseeing before or after the dates of your engagement, and be responsible yourself for any travel or insurance ramifications.

Without a safety net

The British Council by no means has the monopoly on overseas touring, and your independent producer or tour booker may have their own network to promote you. More risky is attempting to set up your own foreign touring, and Mark Makin has some helpful advice about it. He suggests that if the promoter overseas does not insist on seeing your play live, they will at least want a representative to vet your show, or to have a copy of that full-length DVD.

Extra care will need to be taken over the details of your contract, as misunderstandings are less easily resolved away from home territory. As well as the currency and the size of the fee, you must negotiate provision for air or sea travel, excess baggage if required, work permits or visas where stipulated, suitable accommodation, transfers and internal travel and, in the case of transporting stage or technical equipment, the freight costs both there and back. (On a recent Far East tour, Mark had covered every contingency except the latter – return freighting of a set and costumes – and the resultant cost wiped out his profit entirely.)

Be certain that you have adequate insurance cover. Check, too, that you are not liable for withholding tax in the countries you visit, as these can be exorbitant and similarly diminish your profit. To avoid confusion and panic at your technical rehearsals you should reassure yourself that there will be a technician at your overseas venue with a good command of both written and spoken English. And if you'll be doing press or other media interviews to promote the show it's important that a translator be present to help you and your interviewer.

Mark's final exhortation is that you should not board the plane to take off on your overseas adventure unless you have cleared funds in your bank account for fifty per cent of your fee. This is a quite standard arrangement, and if the contract is signed months before the engagement and half the fee safely banked away it can really help with your cash flow.

Postscript

You'll have noted different patterns of behaviour in the actors – and their solo shows – described earlier. There are the flirters who bond with their subject briefly and then return to the sanity of a conventional career. There are the long-term monogamous monologists who stay in partnership with their one subject for a number of years before an amicable parting of the ways. Then at the other extreme are the serial solo players who may have half-a-dozen different shows which they have coupled with, and drop sequentially in order to take up with a new one, or keep in a repertoire to be visited, like a harem, when desired.

The latter group will mostly admit that, like a writer's second novel, it is the second solo show that proves the hardest nut to crack. Having made a success of the first one, and learnt from your mistakes, there is no guarantee that a similar formula will work again, or that the obstacles and challenges will be the same, or solvable by the same means. Like the character of Philip Henslowe says in Marc Norman and Tom Stoppard's screenplay for *Shakespeare in Love*: 'It's a mystery.' But at the heart of the mystery is most likely the ingredient that inspired you to fly solo in the first place: passion.

Appendices

WEBSITES REFERENCED IN THE BOOK

Money

The Acting Website www.theactingwebsite.com

Arts Council England www.artscouncil.org.uk

Arts and Business www.artsandbusiness.org.uk

National Lottery Funding www.lotteryfunding.org.uk

Association of Charitable Foundations www.acf.org.uk

People

Doollee www.doollee.com

PRS for Music www.prsformusic.com

Dance UK www.danceuk.org

Stage Jobs Pro www.uk.stagejobspro.com

Equity www.equity.org.uk

Festivals/Touring

Edinburgh Festival Fringe www.edfringe.com

Edinburgh Festival Flats www.festivalflats.net

British Arts Festivals Association www.artsfestivals.co.uk

National Rural Touring Forum www.nrtf.org.uk

British Council www.britishcouncil.org

Admin/Producing

HM Revenue and Customs www.hmrc.gov.uk (re. tax)

Criminal Records Bureau www.crb.gov.uk (re. criminal record checks)

FUNDING

Arts Council England www.artscouncil.org.uk

Arts Council of Northern Ireland www.artscouncil-ni.org

Arts Council of Wales www.artswales.org.uk

Creative Scotland (formerly Arts Council Scotland)
www.creativescotland.com

Awards for All www.awardsforall.org.uk

The Big Lottery Fund www.biglotteryfund.org.uk

Heritage Lottery Fund www.hlf.org.uk

Trusts and Foundation

Calouste Gulbenkian Foundation www.gulbenkian.org.uk
The foundation supports original projects, particularly those
which take place outside London. Their arts funding programme
is mainly for professional arts organisations or professional artists
working in partnerships or groups. Its purpose is to support the
development of new art in any artform. It does not cover activities
which are linked to mainstream education. The foundation
welcomes applications from British-based organisations involving
work with international artists.

Esmée Fairbairn Foundation www.esmeefairbairn.org.uk
The foundation is one of the largest independent foundations that
provide grants in the UK. Approximately 75% of its Arts &
Heritage grants budget go to the arts and 25% to heritage projects.

The Peter De Haan Charitable Trust www.pdhct.org.uk
Grants are awarded to organisations that provide opportunities to take part in the arts in educational and community settings, especially for people or groups with limited access to the arts.

The Clore Duffield Foundation www.cloreduffield.org.uk
The foundation concentrates its support on education, the arts, museum and gallery education, health, social care and disability, placing a particular emphasis on supporting children, young people and more vulnerable people such as people with learning disabilities.

The Foyle Foundation www.foylefoundation.org.uk
The foundation is an independent trust that gives grants to UK charities whose main work is in the areas of learning, arts and health. Its priorities are to help make the arts more accessible by developing new audiences, supporting tours, festivals and arts education projects, encouraging new work, and supporting young and emerging artists.

The Paul Hamlyn Foundation www.phf.org.uk
The arts programme encourages new ways for people in the UK to enjoy, experience and be involved in the arts. Funding benefits organisations and groups through the grants scheme and special projects.

The Directory of Social Change (DSC) www.dsc.org.uk
Includes a link to funding resource websites. The DSC publishes several funding guides and handbooks.

Business Funding

Business Link www.businesslink.gov.uk
Business Link is a national service giving advice to businesses. It has several offices around the country. The website contains information and links to local agencies.

The Prince's Trust www.princes-trust.org.uk
The Prince's Trust provides training, financial help, grants and other support for people aged fourteen to thirty.

Career Development Loans
www.direct.gov.uk/en/EducationAndLearning/Adult
Learning/CareerDevelopmentLoans
Career Development Loans gives people help to fund vocational
education or learning through a loan. The service is run by three
national banks on behalf of the Government.

Overseas Funding

The following organisations can provide information and
advice on funding for activities taking place outside of the UK
or for overseas artists looking to bring their work to the UK.

EUCLID www.euclid.info
EUCLID provides information, research and consultancy
services. EUCLID also provides support and help for those
applying to the European Union's funding scheme for arts and
culture, as well as guidance on other EU funding opportunities.
The website contains free, downloadable information on sources
of funding from the European Union.

Visiting Arts www.visitingarts.org.uk
Visiting Arts is a national agency for promoting the flow of
international arts into the UK and developing related cultural
links. The agency runs a number of schemes for international
artists visiting the UK. Funding is aimed at UK-based promoters
and venues who invite overseas artists and art projects.

International Intelligence on Culture www.intelculture.org
International Intelligence on Culture is an independent organisation
specialising in consultancy, research, project management, training
and advisory services relating to international projects.

Useful Organisations

Organisations, directories and websites you may find useful in
your search for funding. Some of the organisations listed can
provide advice and information on funding opportunities,
and others offer support for professional fundraisers.

Association of Charitable Foundations (ACF)
www.acf.org.uk
ACF is the leading association for charities in the UK who provide grants. ACF also provides a list of trusts and charities. The website contains extra advice on applying for grants.

Institute of Fundraising www.institute-offundraising.org.uk
The Institute of Fundraising is the professional body that represents fundraisers in the UK. Their mission is to help fundraisers provide excellent fundraising

Arts and Business www.artsandbusiness.org.uk
Through twelve regional offices, A&B helps businesses and arts organisations to come together to create partnerships to benefit themselves and the community. A&B publishes books and directories on sponsorship in the arts.

FunderFinder www.funderfinder.org.uk
FunderFinder is a small UK charity producing software and other resources, mainly for those looking for grants. Some of the services are free, some are not, though many people use the software at no cost in a library or resource agency.

Useful Websites

Funders' Site www.fundersonline.org

UK Fundraising www.fundraising.co.uk

Idox www.j4b.co.uk

Charities Direct www.charitiesdirect.com

EU Cultural Contact Point www.culturefund.eu

PRODUCERS AND AGENTS

A selection of UK producers, tour bookers and tour managers who work with solo performers

makin projects www.makinprojects.co.uk

Richardson PR & Management
www.richardsonprm.com

Scamp www.scamptheatre.com

Seabright Productions Ltd
www.seabrightproductions.co.uk

Theatre Tours International
www.theatretoursinternational.com

UK Arts International www.ukarts.com

Agencies that represent playwrights

The Agency (London) Ltd www.theagency.co.uk

Alan Brodie Representations Ltd www.alanbrodie.com

Berlin Associates www.berlinassociates.com

Casarotto, Ramsay and Associates Ltd
www.casarotto.co.uk

Curtis Brown Group Ltd www.curtisbrown.co.uk

Judy Daish Associates Ltd www.judydaish.com

David Higham Associates www.davidhigham.co.uk

Independent Talent Group Ltd (formerly ICM)
www.independenttalent.com

The Knight Hall Agency Ltd www.knighthallagency.com

Micheline Steinberg Associates www.steinplays.com

Julia Tyrrell Management www.jtmanagement.com

United Agents www.unitedagents.co.uk

VENUES

UK venues that take solo work (by Arts Council region)

East

Bedford School Theatre, Bedford, MK40 2TU
www.bedfordschool.org.uk/theatre

Chelmsford Theatres, Chelmsford, CM1 1JG
www.chelmsford.gov.uk/theatres

Hat Factory, Luton, LU1 2EY www.thehatfactory.org

Maltings Arts Theatre, St Albans, AL1 3HL
www.stalbans.gov.uk/mat

New Wolsey Theatre, Ipswich, IP1 2AS
www.wolseytheatre.co.uk

Playhouse, Harlow, CM20 1LS
www.playhouseharlow.com

Playhouse, Norwich, NR3 1AB
www.norwichplayhouse.org.uk

Quay Theatre, Sudbury, CO10 6AN
www.quaytheatre.org.uk

Theatre Royal, Bury St. Edmunds, IP33 1QR
www.theatreroyal.org

East Midlands

Blackfriars Arts Centre, Boston, PE21 6HP
www.blackfriarsartscentre.co.uk

Castle, Wellingborough, NN8 1XA www.thecastle.org.uk

Curve, Leicester, LE1 1SB www.curveonline.co.uk

Drill Hall, Lincoln, LN2 1EY www.lincolndrillhall.com

Guildhall Arts Centre, Derby, DE1 3AH
www.derbylive.co.uk

Guildhall Arts Centre, Grantham, NG31 6PZ
www.guildhallartscentre.com

Lakeside Arts Centre, Nottingham, NG7 2RD
www.lakesidetower.co.uk

Palace Theatre, Newark, NG24 1JY
www.palacenewark.com

South Holland Centre, Spalding, PE11 1SS
www.southhollandcentre.co.uk

Stamford Arts Centre, Stamford, PE9 2BN
www.stamfordartscentre.com

Town Hall, Loughborough, LE11 3EB
www.loughboroughtownhall.co.uk

London

Arts Centre, Harrow, HA5 4EA www.harrowarts.com

Artsdepot, London, N12 0GA www.artsdepot.co.uk

Jackson's Lane, London, N6 5AA www.jacksonslane.org.uk

Redbridge Drama Centre, South Woodford, E18 2RB
www.redbridgedramacentre.co.uk

Rich Mix, Bethnal Green, E1 6LA www.richmix.org.uk

North East

Arc, Stockton-on-Tees, TS18 1LL www.arconline.co.uk

Darlington Arts Centre, Darlington, DL3 7AX
www.darlington.gov.uk/arts

Playhouse, Alnwick, NE66 1PQ
www.alnwickplayhouse.co.uk

Queen's Hall Arts, Hexham, NE46 3LS
www.queenshall.co.uk

North West

Brewery Arts Centre, Cumbria, LA9 4HE
www.breweryarts.co.uk

Brindley, Runcorn, WA7 1BG
www.halton.gov.uk/thebrindley

Burnley Mechanics, Burnley, BB11 1JA
www.burnleymechanics.co.uk

Dukes, Lancaster, LA1 1QE www.dukes-lancaster.org

Forum 28, Barrow-in-Furness, LA14 1HU
www.forumtwentyeight.co.uk

Met, Bury, BL9 0BW www.themet.biz

Rosehill Theatre, Whitehaven, CA28 6SE
www.rosehilltheatre.co.uk

Theatre by the Lake, Keswick, CA12 5DJ
www.theatrebythelake.com

Unity Theatre, Liverpool, L1 9EG
www.unitytheatreliverpool.co.uk

Wave, Maryport, CA15 8AD
www.thewavemaryport.co.uk

Scotland

Arts Centre, Paisley, PA1 2BA
www.renfrewshire.gov.uk/ilwwcm/publishing.nsf/Content
/els-PaisleyArtsCentre-ArtsandMuseums

Brunton Theatre, Musselburgh, EH21 6AA
www.bruntontheatre.co.uk

Byre Theatre, St Andrews, KY16 9LA
www.byretheatre.com

Eastgate Theatre, Peebles, EH45 8AD www.eastgatearts.com

Eastwood Park Theatre, Glasgow, G46 6UG
www.eastwoodparktheatre.co.uk

Hamilton Town House, Hamilton, ML3 6HH
www.southlanarkshire.gov.uk

Lemon Tree, Aberdeen, AB24 5AT
www.boxofficeaberdeen.com

MacRobert, Stirling, FK9 4LA www.macrobert.org

Maltings, Berwick-upon-Tweed, TD15 1DT
www.maltingsberwick.co.uk

South East

Ashcroft Arts Centre, Fareham, PO16 7DX
www3.hants.gov.uk/ashcroft

Brook Theatre, Chatham, ME4 4SE
www.medway.gov.uk/theatres

Camberley Theatre, Camberley, GU15 3SY
www.camberleytheatre.biz

Corn Exchange, Newbury, RG14 5BD
www.cornexchangenew.com

Cornerstone, Didcot, OX11 7NE
www.cornerstone-arts.org

Forest Arts Centre, New Milton, BH25 6DS
www.forest-arts.co.uk

Gulbenkian Theatre, Canterbury, CT2 7NB
www.kent.ac.uk/gulbenkian

Hawth Studio, Crawley, RH10 6YZ www.hawth.co.uk

Lights, Andover, SP10 1AH www.thelights.org.uk

Limelight Theatre, Aylesbury, HP21 7RT www.qpc.org

New Theatre Royal, Portsmouth, PO1 2DD
www.newtheatreroyal.com

Norden Farm Centre for the Arts, Maidenhead, SL6 4PF
www.nordenfarm.org

Nuffield Theatre, Southampton, SO9 5NH
www.nuffieldtheatre.co.uk

Point, Eastleigh, SO50 9DE www.thepointeastleigh.co.uk

Quay Arts Centre, Newport Harbour, PO30 5BD
www.quayarts.org

South Hill Park Arts Centre, Bracknell, RG12 7PA
www.southhillpark.org.uk

South Street Arts Centre, Reading, RG1 4QR
www.readingarts.com/southstreet

Spring Arts and Heritage Centre, Havant, PO9 1BS
www.thespring.co.uk

Theatre Royal, Margate, CT9 1PW
www.theatreroyalmargate.com

The Theatre, Chipping Norton, OX7 5NL
www.chippingnortontheatre.co.uk

Winchester Discovery Centre, Winchester, SO23 8RX
www3.hants.gov.uk/wdc.htm

South West

Arc Theatre, Trowbridge, BA14 OES
www.arctheatre.org.uk

Arts Centre, Salisbury, SP1 3UT
www.salisburyartscentre.co.uk

Arts Centre, Swindon, SN1 4BJ
www.swindon.gov.uk/artscentre

Brewhouse Theatre, Taunton, TA1 4JL
www.thebrewhouse.net

Crediton Arts Centre, Crediton, EX17 3AX
www.creditonartscentre.org

Flavel, Dartmouth, TQ6 9ND www.theflavel.org.uk

Jersey Arts Centre, Jersey JE2 4SW
www.thisisjersey.co.uk/jac

Merlin Theatre, Frome, BA11 2HQ
www.merlintheatre.co.uk

Phoenix Arts Centre, Exeter, EX4 3LS
www.exeterphoenix.org.uk

Plough Arts Centre, Great Torrington, EX38 8HQ
www.plough-arts.org

Roses Theatre, Tewkesbury, GL20 5NX
www.rosestheatre.org

Tobacco Factory, Bristol, BS3 1TF
www.tobaccofactory.com

Wales

Aberystwyth Arts Centre, Aberystwyth, SY23 3DE
www.aberystwythartscentre.co.uk

Borough Theatre, Abergavenny, NP7 5HD
www.boroughtheatreabergavenny.co.uk

Riverfront, Newport, NP20 1HG
www.newport.gov.uk/theriverfront

Taliesen Arts Centre, Swansea, SA2 8PZ
www.taliesinartscentre.co.uk

Theatr Clwyd, Mold, CH7 1YA
www.clwyd-theatr-cymru.co.uk

Theatr Gwaun, Fishguard, SA65 9AD
www.pembrokeshire.gov.uk

Theatr Hafren, Newtown, SY16 1BE www.theatrhafren.com

Theatr Mwldan, Cardigan, SA43 1JY www.mwldan.co.uk

Torch Theatre, Milford Haven, SA73 2BU
www.torchtheatre.co.uk

Wyeside Arts Centre, Builth Wells, LD2 3AH
www.wyeside.co.uk

West Midlands

Arena Theatre, Wolverhampton, WV1 1SB
www.arena.wlv.ac.uk

Artrix, Bromsgrove, B60 1AX www.artrix.co.uk

Assembly Rooms, Ludlow, SY8 1AZ
www.ludlowassemblyrooms.co.uk

Belgrade Theatre, Coventry, CV1 1GS
www.belgrade.co.uk

Courtyard, Hereford, HR4 9JR www.thecourtyard.org.uk

Garrick, Lichfield, WS13 6HR www.lichfieldgarrick.com

Gatehouse Theatre, Stafford, ST16 2LT
www.staffordgatehousetheatre.co.uk

mac, Birmingham, B12 9QH www.macarts.co.uk

Oakengates Theatre, Telford, TF2 6EP
www.oakengates.ws

Old Town Hall Arts Centre, Hemel Hempstead, HP1 3AE
www.dacorum.gov.uk/arts

Solihull Arts Complex, Solihull, B99 3RG
www.solihull.gov.uk

UH Arts, Hatfield, AL10 9EU www.herts.ac.uk

Warwick Arts Centre, Coventry, CV4 7AL
www.warwickartscentre.co.uk

Yorkshire

Civic, Barnsley, S70 2JL www.barnsleycivic.co.uk

Doncaster Civic Theatre, Doncaster, DN1 3ET
www.doncastercivic.co.uk

Georgian Theatre Royal, Richmond, DL10 4DW
www.georgiantheatreroyal.co.uk

Harrogate Theatre, Harrogate, HG1 1QF
www.harrogatetheatre.co.uk

Hull Truck Theatre, Hull, HU2 8RW
www.hulltruck.co.uk

Lawrence Batley Theatre (LBT), Huddersfield, HD1 2SP
www.thelbt.org

Rotherham Civic Theatre, Rotherham, S65 1EB
www.rotherham.gov.uk/theatres

FESTIVALS

Aberdeen International Youth Festival (July–August)
www.aiyf.org

Bridlington Arts Festival, Yorkshire (May)
www.bridlingtonartsfestival.com

Bromsgrove Festival, Worcestershire (April–May)
www.bromsgrovefestival.co.uk

Bury St Edmunds Festival, Suffolk (May)
www.buryfestival.co.uk

Buxton Festival (& Fringe Festival), Derbyshire (July)
www.buxtonfestival.co.uk

Canterbury Festival, Kent (October)
www.canterburyfestival.co.uk

Chelsea Arts Festival, London (June)
www.chelseaartsfestival.org

Chichester Festivities, West Sussex (July)
www.chifest.org.uk

Corsham Festival, Wiltshire (June)
www.corshamfestival.org.uk

Earagail Arts Festival, Co Donegal (July) www.eaf.ie

Edinburgh Festival Fringe (August) www.edfringe.com

Frome Festival, Somerset (July) www.fromefestival.co.uk

Grassington Festival of Music and Arts, Yorkshire
(June–July) www.grassington-festival.org.uk

Gwyl Gregynog Festival, Wales (June–July)
www.gwylgregynogfestival.org

Halesworth Arts Festival, Suffolk (October)
www.halesworthartsfestival.org.uk

Hampstead and Highgate Festival, London
(September–October) www.hamandhighfest.co.uk

Hebden Bridge Arts Festival, Yorkshire (June–July)
www.hebdenbridgeartsfestival.co.uk

Henley Festival, Oxfordshire (July)
www.henley-festival.co.uk

Hexham Abbey Festival, Northumberland
(September–October) www.hexhamabbey.org.uk/festival

Holloway Arts Festival, London (June–July)
www.hollowayartsfestival.co.uk

Holt Summer Festival, Norfolk (July)
www.holtsummerfestival.org

Leamington Peace Festival, Warwickshire (August)
www.peacefestival.org.uk

Lichfield Festival, Staffordshire (July)
www.lichfieldfestival.org

Little Missenden Festival, Buckinghamshire (October)
www.little-missenden.org

Ludlow Festival, Shropshire (July)
www.ludlowfestival.co.uk

Macclesfield Barnaby Festival, Cheshire (June)
www.barnabyfestival.org.uk

Mananan International Festival of Music & the Arts, Isle
of Man (June–July) www.erinartscentre.com

Mole Valley Arts Alive Festival, Surrey (October)
www.arts-alive.co.uk

Much Wenlock Festival Society (June)
www.muchwenlockfestival.co.uk

Norfolk & Norwich Festival (May) www.nnfestival.org.uk

Northern Aldborough Festival, Yorkshire (June)
www.aldborough.com/festival

Pembroke Festival, Wales (July)
www.pembrokefestival.org.uk

Petworth Festival, Surrey (July)
www.petworthfestival.org.uk

Portsmouth Festivities, Hampshire (June)
www.portsmouthfestivities.co.uk

Rye Festival, East Sussex (September)
www.ryeartsfestival.co.uk

Ryedale Festival, Yorkshire (July)
www.ryedalefestival.co.uk

Salisbury International Arts Festival, Wiltshire
(May–June) www.salisburyfestival.co.uk

Spitalfields Summer Festival, London (June)
www.spitalfieldsfestival.org.uk

Tenby Arts Festival, Wales (September)
www.tenbyartsfest.co.uk

Wirksworth Arts Festival, Derbyshire (September)
www.wirksworthfestival.co.uk

Worcester Festival, Worcestershire (August)
www.worcesterfestival.co.uk

Arts Out West, Cumbria artsoutwest@thekirkgate.com

Artsreach, Dorset info@artsreach.co.uk

Beaford Arts, Devon hannah@beaford-arts.org.uk

Black Country Touring us@bctouring.co.uk

Carn to Cove, Cornwall admin@actcornwall.org.uk

Cheshire's Rural Arts Network
prescottsmith@cheshirewestandchester.gov.uk

Durham Touring, Durham neil.hillier@durham.gov.uk

Essex On Tour tony.morrison@essex.gov.uk

Farnham Maltings Touring, Hampshire
janice.brittain@farnhammaltings.com

Hog the Limelight, Hampshire nadine.fry@hants.gov.uk

Lincolnshire Rural and Community Touring
sue.beresford@nottscc.gov.uk

Live & Local, Derbyshire admin@liveandlocal.org.uk

Making Tracks, West Sussex
Karen.Howard@westsussex.gov.uk

Midlands (East) sue@artservice.org.uk

Midlands (West) sian@artsalive.co.uk

Northants Touring Arts, Nottingham
info@northantstouringarts.co.uk

Oxfordshire Rural and Community Touring
nicola.riley@cherwell-dc.gov.uk

Razzle, South Gloucester neenmcbeen@gmail.com

Rural Arts Wiltshire info@ruralartswiltshire.org.uk

Spot On – Lancashire Touring Network
hello@spotonlancashire.co.uk

Take Art! Somerset sarah@takeart.org

Theatre in the Villages, Buckinghamshire
dclucas@aylesburyvaledc.gov.uk

Village Ventures Nottinghamshire
sue.beresford@nottscc.gov.uk

Villages in Action, Devon roger@villagesinaction.co.uk

INSURANCE

For a solo performer, Equity seem to give the best comprehensive insurance as part of their annual membership fee. If you have an extensive set and/or props then you may need to take out insurance that covers theft from a locked room (venues/hotel/B&B accommodation) and a locked van (if you tour in a van). Contact www.equity.org.uk for further information.

If you employ a technician to operate your show you should ensure that they carry adequate personal, and public liability insurance.

Established Theatrical Insurers

First Act Insurance www.firstact.co.uk

Gordon & Co. www.firststepinsurance.co.uk

RATES OF PAY

ITC Guidelines can be accessed at www.itc-arts.org. The 2011 rates of pay were as follows:

Writers

Full-length play	£7,328
Play under 70 minutes in length	£4,886
Play under 30 minutes in length	£2,443
Minimum royalty (Clause I 7.2)	£50
Royalty threshold (Clause II A.3)	£49,372
Meal allowance (Clause II A.4c)	£14.20
Management participation threshold (Clause II A.5)	£28,211.50
Additional day rate (Clause II B.2vii)	£54
Pre/post show discussions (Clause II B.2xi)	£54
Option purchase (Clause II C.4b)	£705

Directors

Director's fee (full-length play)	£1305
Director's fee (short-length play)	£903
Weekly exclusive services payment	£400
Artistic/Resident Directors	£485

FURTHER READING

These are useful American publications, all available via Amazon.

Acting Solo: The Art of the One-man Shows by Jordon R. Young (Moonstone Press)

Creating Your Own Monologue by Glenn Alterman (Allworth Press)

Getting Your Solo Act Together by Michael Kearns (Heinemann)

The Power of One: The Solo Play for Playwrights, Actors and Directors by Loius E. Catron (Heinemann)

The Solo Performer's Journey: From the Page to the Stage by Michael Kearns (Heinemann)

Your Name Here: An Actor/Writers' Guide to Solo Performance by Susan Merson (Star Publish)